THE WALK SERIES

A LAMP UNTO MY FEET

A 12-WEEK STUDY THROUGH PSALM 119

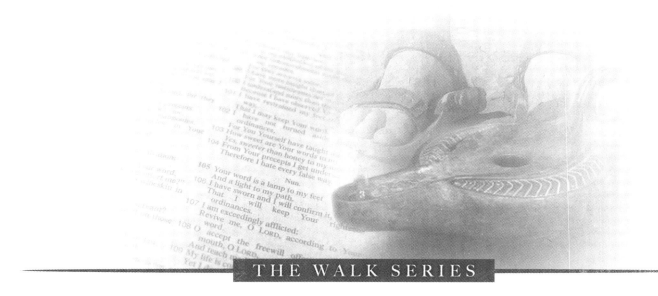

THE WALK SERIES

A LAMP UNTO MY FEET

A 12-WEEK STUDY THROUGH PSALM 119

STEVE GALLAGHER

"Purity for Life"

www.purelifeministries.org

888.PURELIFE

Also available by Pure Life Ministries:

At the Altar of Sexual Idolatry
A Biblical Guide to Counseling the Sexual Addict
Create in Me a Pure Heart
From Ashes to Beauty
He Leads Me Beside Still Waters
How America Lost Her Innocence
Intoxicated with Babylon
Irresistible to God
Living in Victory
Out of the Depths of Sexual Sin
Pressing On Toward the Heavenly Calling
Standing Firm through the Great Apostasy
The Walk of Repentance

For these books and other teaching materials please contact:

Pure Life Ministries

14 School Street
Dry Ridge, KY 41035
(888) PURELIFE - to order
(859) 824-4444
(859) 813-0005 FAX
www.purelifeministries.org

EAN 978-0-9758832-5-9
ISBN 0-9758832-5-9

www.purelifeministries.org
888.PURELIFE

I dedicate this book to every believer who loves and
reverences the Word of God.

Special thanks to:

Ed & Karla Buch, Scott Cochran, Marshall Bradley,
Bob Asmus, Bill & Judy Lucas, Robert Reschar,
Ken Terry, John Delmon, and Carol Smider
for their invaluable aid in putting this Bible study together.

A Lamp Unto My Feet

CONTENTS

INTRODUCTION

Every true believer, having been "rescued from the domain of darkness," is now moving, day by day, toward his eternal, heavenly destination. "And the city has no need of the sun or of the moon to shine on it," John wrote; "for the glory of God has illumined it, and its lamp is the Lamb." (Revelation 21:23) Scripture further tells us, "God is Light" (I John 1:5) and "dwells in unapproachable light." (I Timothy 6:15-16) Yes, one day believers will leave this dark planet and cross the shimmering sea that leads to "the city of the living God." (Hebrews 12:22)

However, before making that final crossing into the land of immortality, the Christian pilgrim must first travel through the gloomy morass of a malevolently hostile empire. Scripture tells us this "world lies in the power of the evil one." (I John 5:19) Thus, it is a journey fraught with "dangers, toils and snares." Even believers are highly susceptible to the influences of this dark lord who tirelessly attempts to deceive, pollute and lure into sin. How will they find their way through this land of malignant shadows?

Fortunately, the "Father of lights" has not left His children to fend for themselves but rather has provided a roadmap—a marvelous glory-book written by inspired men who witnessed this Kingdom of Light through firsthand experience. Little wonder that David* christened it *A Lamp Unto My Feet.* Anyone who has stumbled through the black night of the Negev desert (where the young shepherd spent many nights) intimately comprehends the significance of such a title. David understood his great need for the wisdom, insights and continual guidance of Scripture to safely complete his own journey.

Oh, how I pity those who show little concern over the eternal dangers they face and do not grasp the gravity of this Book of Light. Think of it! THE… WORD… OF… GOD. Does the wonder of it still thrill your soul…….or has it become a tired, lifeless collection of worn-out instructions to you? Do you

ever erupt in praise as Paul did when he exclaimed, "Oh, the depth of the riches both of the wisdom and knowledge of God! How unsearchable are His judgments and unfathomable His ways!" Or has the indulgence of worldly charms dulled your spiritual senses to its brilliance?

Dear one, however much we may esteem or disdain it, the Bible towers above every other book ever written. Its spiritual truths are incomprehensible when approached with a purely academic mindset. Of course, kept in its proper place, scholastic study of Scripture has certain usefulness. Researching historical data about the customs and manners of the ancient world can provide valuable insights into the lives of biblical characters and so on. But the Bible is much more than a divinely inspired history book. It is also much more than a compilation of rules to live by or even a trustworthy source of biblical counseling.

As much as religious people** resist the fact, the Bible breathes the very life of God. "The word of God is living and active…" (Hebrews 4:12) It does not open itself to the calculating deductions of the fallen human intellect***.

The deep spiritual truths found in Scripture can only be grasped as its words are brought to life and illumined by the Holy Spirit. Without the Helper's aid, Scripture can easily digress into a Christianized form of the kind of dry, religious teachings the Pharisees advocated.

I will have considered this Bible study to be a failure—an utter waste of time—if it does not lead the reader into a deeper love, respect and appreciation for God's Word. This goal cannot be achieved simply by looking up a few verses each day. Only the Bible student who has learned to actively seek the aid of the Holy Spirit will bring "out of his treasure things new and old." (Matthew 13:52)

"Unless we realize our dependence upon the Holy Spirit the Word will not speak to us," penned Dr.

---

* Scholars disagree about who actually wrote Psalm 119. For a number of reasons I won't go into, I agree with those who believe it to have been written by David in his younger years. Throughout this study—for the sake of simplicity—I will treat him as the author.

** Those who attempt to keep their Christian faith within the controllable boundaries of human reasoning and experience.

*** Matthew 11:25

Introduction - continued

Martyn Lloyd-Jones. "If we read the Word of God without praying for enlightenment, we shall probably get very little out of it. We must never depart from this consciousness of our dependence upon the Spirit's power and enlightenment. The 'anointing', the 'unction from the Holy One', of which the Apostle John speaks is needed constantly and increasingly."[1]

With that in mind, I would like to offer a few suggestions that I believe will help the reader maximize the benefits of this study through Psalm 119:

First, prayerfully approach each day's lessons. The Lord will speak to you and implant His wisdom in your heart if you will but ask Him. You do not need more biblical knowledge; you need a divine impartation! If you will ask, seek and knock, unexpected doors will be opened to you through Scripture. Approach the Word with expectancy and faith!

Second, be ever mindful that you live in a world that lies under a satanic enchantment. Spiritual darkness pervades our culture. The intoxicating voice of darkness blares at you relentlessly through television, radio and the Internet. It appears as truth, but is actually laced with underlying false messages, cunningly cloaked in seemingly innocuous information. The Bible is the one existing source of pure *truth*. Humble yourself before it and treat it with the utmost reverence.

Third, spend as much time as you can in your studies. You probably don't realize how much you have been polluted by the spirit of this world.[5****] The more time you spend soaking in Scripture, the more you will take on the mind of God. Conversely, the more you immerse yourself in the world, the more its standards and values will shape your thinking and desires.

If you feel as though you have already been terribly contaminated, don't despair! The Word of God can and will straighten out faulty perspectives, skewed attitudes and unlawful desires. You need only immerse yourself in it, allowing it to do its supernatural work inside you. David said it himself: "The law of the Lord is perfect, restoring the soul..." (Psalm 19:7)

**** For an exhaustive study on how the spirit of this world is affecting believers, please see my book, *Intoxicated with Babylon*.

Last, please keep in mind that Psalm 119 was written by a man with a great love for Scripture. To the spiritually dull, and those who are devoted to worldly entertainment, spending time in it will seem like a tedious, obligatory drudgery. To those who approach this study with a grateful, loving heart, it will become a "fountain of life."

Practical Considerations

Before you begin, there are a few pertinent items to consider about the study. Each week (with the exception of the first and last) will cover two eight-verse stanzas of Psalm 119. Notice also that each day offers a supplemental reading: pertinent Psalms recommended for those who want to spend more time studying after completing the daily lesson. Occasionally, you will be asked to look up a Hebrew word in a Bible dictionary. This can be a thorough reference book such as the *Theological Wordbook of the Old Testament*, *Vine's Expository Dictionary*, or the simpler *Strong's Hebrew Dictionary* found on many computer Bible programs. To assist you in this, the Strong's reference numbers have been provided throughout in these instances.

In most of the Friday studies, I offer different Bible translations which provide a fresh perspective on key verses for that week's study. The following are a list of the versions utilized: *The Amplified Bible* (AMP), *The Living Bible* (LIV), *New Living Translation* (NLT) *The New Testament in Basic English* (BAS), *The Psalms for Today* (HAR), *The Jerusalem Bible* (JER), *Contemporary English Version* (CEV) *The New English Bible* (NEB) *The Bible in Basic English* (BBE), *The Good News Bible* (GNB), and the *Jewish Publication Society Bible* (JPS).

The purpose of Saturday's homework is to challenge the reader to personally apply what he or she has learned from the week's lessons (which explains why the questions may, at times, seem disjointed). Sundays will be devoted to studying the life of David, the first two reports focusing on Samuel and Saul—the two most influential men in his life.

Finally, I want to encourage you to put your heart into each day's lesson. For instance, when you are asked to look up various passages and tell what

Introduction - continued

you learn from them, try to resist the temptation to impatiently rewrite what has been stated. Think about what is being expressed in that verse, carefully pondering each word. Consider the verse in light of the passage in Psalm 119 you are studying. Most of all, prayerfully ask the Lord to open the Word to your heart.

It is my hope that, as you prayerfully work your way through *A Lamp Unto My Feet*, it will prove to be a true blessing to you. My prayer is that it will stir up a greater hunger within you to know God, understand His ways, and live in submission to His will. May the truths you uncover during the next twelve weeks deepen your love for this amazing treasure—God's holy Word!

WEEK 1: STRAIGHT AND NARROW

Monday

1. Please read the following introduction to Psalm 119 and follow the instructions provided. (supplemental reading: Psalm 14)

Psalm 119 is unique in the Bible, both in its length (it is more than twice as long as its closest rival Psalm) and its symmetry, being laid out to coincide with the 22 letters of the Hebrew alphabet. Each stanza consists of 8 verses; each verse within that stanza begins with the same Hebrew letter. Thus, the first eight verses begin with the letter "a" (Heb. aleph), the second group all begin with the letter "b" (Heb. beth), and so on. With the exception of one or two, every verse in this great Psalm speaks of the Word of God.

Admittedly, the superficial reader can easily become bored with Psalm 119. It can seem as though David was being painfully redundant in his writing. But the thoughtful reader will pick up on the subtle nuances of each sentence. This Psalm was not written as a doctrinal teaching (i.e. Romans) but as a prayer. In it, David discusses the blessings of obedience, the importance of meditation, his commitment to God's precepts, and most of all, his great reverence and love for the Word of God.

Matthew Henry recounted the following words of advice from his father about this Psalm: "Once, pressing the study of the Scriptures, he advised us to take a verse of this Psalm every morning to meditate upon, and so go over the Psalm twice in the year; 'and that,' saith he, 'will bring you to be in love with all the rest of the Scriptures.' He often said, 'All grace grows as love to the word of God grows.'"

Henry only touched upon the great meaning of Psalm 119. It was written as a prayer from a man who loved the Word but was well aware of his propensity to stray from its precepts. He longed to be kept by the Lord. Psalm 119 is a systematic expression of this cry from his heart, a prayer to be kept on the narrow way as it is laid out in Scripture. If I were to sum up his impassioned cry in a few sentences, it would read something like this:

"Oh Lord, you see my natural tendency to wander away from Your Word. The rebellious disdain your law, but I love everything about it. It is the greatest pleasure of my life to study it, meditate upon it, and pray over its words. Truly it contains the 'words of life.' Please conquer my heart so that I will obey Your precepts. Keep me within the narrow confines of Your judgments. I know I regularly fail, but nevertheless, I commit myself to obeying Your statutes the rest of my life."

Please write out your own prayer of commitment as you commence your study in this magnificent Psalm.

Monday ~ *continued*

2. Look up the following words (which are used throughout this Psalm) in a Bible dictionary and write out the main points mentioned in each definition:

law (Heb. *tôrâh*$_{8451}$):

precepts (Heb. *piqqûd*$_{6490}$):

testimonies (Heb. *'êdâh*$_{5713}$):

way (Heb. *derek*$_{1870}$):

commandments (Heb. *mitsvâh*$_{4687}$):

statutes (Heb. *chôq*$_{2706}$):

word (Heb. *dâbâr*$_{1697}$):

ordinances (or judgments) (Heb. *mishpât*$_{4941}$):

Tuesday

1. Read and meditate on Psalm 119:1-8 (supplemental reading: Psalm 37).

2. Write out Psalm 119:1.

3. Look up the word *blameless* (Heb. *tâmîym*$_{8549}$) in a Bible dictionary and list some of the synonyms provided.

    a.   b.

    c.   d.

    e.   f.

4. Look up the following verses and describe the blessings of being blameless.

    Psalm 37:18-19

    Psalm 84:11

    Proverbs 11:5

    Proverbs 11:20

    Proverbs 28:10

    Proverbs 28:18

Tuesday - continued

5. Read the following commentary and explain what you learn.

Blessed is the man whose life is the practical transcript of the will of God. True religion is not cold and dry; it has its exclamations and raptures. We not only judge the keeping of God's law to be a wise and proper thing, but we are warmly enamored of its holiness, and cry out in adoring wonder, "Blessed are the undefiled!", meaning thereby, that we eagerly desire to become such ourselves, and wish for no greater happiness than to be perfectly holy...

Doubtless, the more complete our sanctification the more intense our blessedness. Christ is our way, and we are not only alive in Christ, but we are to live in Christ: the sorrow is that we bespatter his holy way with our selfishness, self exaltation, willfulness, and carnality, and so we miss a great measure of the blessedness which is in him as our way. A believer who errs is still saved, but the joy of his salvation is not experienced by him; he is rescued but not enriched, greatly borne with, but not greatly blessed...

The law of the Lord is not irksome to them; its commandments are not grievous, and its restrictions are not slavish in their esteem... Nor do they ever regret that they have entered upon the path of obedience, else they would leave it, and that without difficulty, for a thousand temptations offer them opportunity to return; their continued walk in the law of the Lord is their best testimony to the blessedness of such a condition of life... Rough may be the way, stern the rule, hard the discipline—all these we know and more—but a thousand heaped up blessings are still found in godly living, for which we bless the Lord...

Here the Lord, who in the last day will pronounce some to be blessed and some to be cursed, doth now tell us who they are.[1]

Wednesday

1. Read and meditate on Psalm 119:1-8 (supplemental reading: Psalm 34).

2. Write out Psalm 119:2.

3. Look up the word *seek* (Heb. *dârash*[1875]) in a Bible dictionary and rewrite the definition in your own words.

4. Look up the following verses and describe what you learn about this word.

    Deuteronomy 4:29

    Psalm 34:4

    Psalm 34:10

    Psalm 78:34

    Hosea 10:12

Wednesday - *continued*

5. Write out the six clauses of Psalm 119:1-3, which describe how God's blessing comes upon a person's life:

   a. e.g.: whose way is blameless

   b.

   c.

   d.

   e.

   f.

6. Now read the Beatitudes listed in Matthew 5:3-9. Compare the lifestyle being depicted here by Jesus with that by David in today's reading. Describe any similarities you see.

Thursday

1. Read and meditate on Psalm 119:1-8 (supplemental reading: Psalm 15).

2. Write out Psalm 119:4.

3. Look up the word *diligently* (Heb. $m^e\hat{o}d_{3966}$) in a Bible dictionary and list some of the synonyms provided.

   a.   b.

   c.   d.

   e.   f.

4. Write out Psalm 119:4 using each of the synonyms you listed above in place of the word *diligently*.

   a.   e.g., Thou hast ordained Thy precepts, that we should keep them *vehemently*.

   b.

   c.

   d.

   e.

   f.

5. Look up the following verses and describe what you learn from this word ($m^e\hat{o}d$).

   Deuteronomy 4:9

Thursday - continued

Deuteronomy 6:3

Joshua 1:7

Joshua 22:5

Joshua 23:11

6. Explain the difference between half-hearted and diligent obedience.

Friday

1. Read and meditate on Psalm 119:1-8 (supplemental reading: Psalm 53).

2. Write out verses 5 and 6.

3. Living the Christian life requires a cooperative effort on the part of the believer and the Lord. Scripture is full of commandments we are expected to obey. Yet, anyone who attempts to live a life of real obedience to God soon finds out that it is impossible to obey perfectly—no matter how sincerely one tries. A person must have the aid of the Holy Spirit. Look up Mark 9:24 and rewrite this famous phrase about faith, changing it into a cry to obey the Lord.

4. Shame is one of the natural consequences of disobedience. Like one's sense of guilt, it is a healthy mechanism the Lord implanted within the conscience of man, helping to create a sense of conviction over the wrongness of sin. One feels embarrassed over one's failure to do the right thing. In verse 6, David expressed the fact that he feels badly when he does not keep the Lord's statutes. This is the sign of a tender heart. Unfortunately, habitual sin deadens a person's conscience. Look up Proverbs 30:20 and describe the difference between David's heart and this woman's heart.

5. The passage in Psalm 119:1-8 from the Amplified Bible has been provided below. Choose three of these verses where this translation gives you a new perspective or fresh insight and explain what you learn.

    Psalm 119:1. Blessed (happy, fortunate, to be envied) are the undefiled (the upright, truly sincere, and blameless) in the way [of the revealed will of God], who walk (order their conduct and conversation) in the law of the Lord (the whole of God's revealed will).

Friday - continued

Psalm 119:2. Blessed (happy, fortunate, to be envied) are they who keep His testimonies, and who seek, inquire for and of Him and crave Him with the whole heart.

Psalm 119:3. Yes, they do no unrighteousness [no willful wandering from His precepts]; they walk in His ways.

Psalm 119:4. You have commanded us to keep Your precepts, that we should observe them diligently.

Psalm 119:5. Oh, that my ways were directed and established to observe Your statutes [hearing, receiving, loving, and obeying them]!

Psalm 119:6. Then shall I not be put to shame [by failing to inherit Your promises] when I have respect to all Your commandments.

Psalm 119:7. I will praise and give thanks to You with uprightness of heart when I learn [by sanctified experiences] Your righteous judgments [Your decisions against and punishments for particular lines of thought and conduct].

Psalm 119:8. I will keep Your statutes; O forsake me not utterly.

a.

b.

c.

Saturday

1. Read and meditate on Psalm 119:1-8 (supplemental reading: Psalm 12).

2. Reread Tuesday's commentary. Choose four phrases that are meaningful to you and explain why.

3. On a scale of 1 to 10, how would you rate yourself as a seeker after the things of God? Explain your answer.

4. Rewrite each verse in your own words, making it a personal prayer for yourself.

    a. 119:1

    b. 119:2

    c. 119:3

    d. 119:4

    e. 119:5

    f. 119:6

    g. 119:7

    h. 119:8

Sunday

THE PROPHET
I Samuel 2:12-7:17

It had been some three hundred years since Israel had been singularly governed by a national leader. When Joshua died, "there arose another generation after them who did not know the Lord… Then the sons of Israel did evil in the sight of the LORD and served the Baals, and they forsook the LORD…" (Judges 2:10-12)

Over the next three centuries, the Hebrew nation degenerated into a disjointed collection of tribes and clans which often clashed more with each other than with the heathens in their midst. The book of Judges is a record of what could be considered the "Dark Ages" of the Jewish nation. It was a time of chaos and ungodliness, best summed up in two biblical statements: "In those days there was no king in Israel; everyone did what was right in his own eyes." (Judges 21:25) "And word from the LORD was rare in those days, visions were infrequent." (I Samuel 3:1b)

Into this spiritually lawless period, in approximately 1100 B.C., Samuel was born. After weaning him, Hannah fulfilled her promise to deliver her young son to Eli, the high priest. Samuel spent his entire childhood with the old priest of Jehovah, leaving only after Eli had died many years later. Though he was undoubtedly a good man, Eli was a weak father with no control over his two wicked sons.

At that time, Baal worship was a widespread fertility cult in Canaan. Women "worshiped" this demon-god by having sexual relations with the temple priests. Eli's sons, Hophni and Phineas, introduced this same practice into the worship of Jehovah. The Lord eventually sent "a man of God" to confront Eli about his lack of spiritual leadership, rebuking him for honoring his sons above the Lord. Eli should have repented and brought his sons to judgment, but he refused to withstand them.

Young Samuel was forced to grow up in this environment, under the evil influence of these two young mockers. Day in and day out he watched them treat the God of Israel with disdain. One can only imagine the things he witnessed and how all of this must have affected him.

When he was about ten years old, the Lord appeared to Samuel, forewarning of impending judgment coming upon both the land of Israel and its high priest. It is a clear example of something expressed by another prophet, "Surely the Lord GOD does nothing unless He reveals His secret counsel to His servants the prophets." (Amos 3:7) But this was Samuel's first test: would he be faithful to confront the old man whom he loved so much? The young boy did as he was told, prophesying to Eli that his sons would both die on the same day. Again, Eli should have repented of his lack of spiritual leadership, yet he weakly responded, "It is the Lord; let Him do what seems good to Him." (I Samuel 3:18)

Another fifteen years would elapse before the fulfillment of Samuel's prophecy when the Philistines defeated the Israelites in a great battle and took the Ark of the Covenant back to Ashdod. Eli, hearing of this and that his sons had died in the battle, fell over and broke his neck. In one tragic day, the priestly family of Eli was destroyed, leaving 25-year-old Samuel as priest of the land. But by this time, Samuel had already gained a reputation in Israel as the Lord's prophet.

Over the next twenty years, he traveled throughout the land, exhorting the people to turn back to Jehovah, spiritually preparing them to overthrow the Philistines. The greatest day of his life occurred in about 1055 B.C. when he led his people into a great revival, culminated by a crushing defeat of the Philistine army.

The forty-year reign of Philistine terror described in Judges 13:1 had finally come to an end.

During the next few years, the Jewish people enjoyed prosperous peace and, as they had predictably done so many times in the past, gradually drifted away from the Lord. It was about 1050 B.C. when they came to the old prophet demanding a king. And God, as He so often does when stiff-necked people demand what isn't in their best interests, gave them what they wanted.

For Samuel, the newly-appointed monarch would prove to be his greatest source of grief and disappointment in his remaining years.

WEEK 2 : TREASURED IN THE HEART

Monday

1. Read and meditate on Psalm 119:9-16 (supplemental reading: Psalm 41).

2. Write out Psalm 119:9-11.

3. Now rewrite verses 9-11 into a single statement in your own words. As you do so, answer the question posed in verse 9, again in your own words.

4. Read the excerpt below and answer the questions on the following page.

    Jesus turned to them and said, "Now you Pharisees clean the outside of the cup and of the platter; but inside of you, you are full of robbery and wickedness. You foolish ones, did not He who made the outside make the inside also? But give that which is within as charity, and then all things are clean for you," (Luke 11:39-41).

    I have dealt with thousands of men in sexual sin over the last fifteen years. Many had learned to clean the outward life. They faithfully attended church. They quit their past life of partying and carousing. They had repented of the open rebellion they had once lived in toward God. Outwardly they seemed to be doing fairly well. However, it was another matter inwardly…

    Jesus did not scold the Pharisees for cleaning up their outward lives. It is pleasing to God for us to go to church and to repent of that outward visible evidence of wickedness. He was trying to teach them that it is just as important to cleanse the inside life as well. Many men who have been controlled by a driving lust have managed to overcome the outward acts of sexual sin, but are still consumed by lust inside. Something must change in the inward life.

    Jesus gave the answer to the Pharisees that day. "…give that which is within as charity, and then all things are clean for you." In that one word He put His finger right on the problem. In their hearts the Pharisees were not givers but takers.… .

    In that one word, giving, He provides the answer to the person who has learned how to do the outward things of religion and yet is still filled with wickedness. This one word, which is used some two thousand times in Scripture, describes the fundamental nature of God and consequently what it means to be godly. It also describes why many remain defeated.[1]

Monday - *continued*

a. What do you think Jesus meant when He inferred that there was a difference between the outward behavior of the Pharisees and what went on inside them?

b. Explain the importance of what occurs inside a person's heart concerning the issue of moral purity.

c. What do you think Jesus meant when He said that giving is the answer to inward pollution? Explain your answer.

Tuesday

1. Read and meditate on Psalm 119:9-16 (supplemental reading: Psalm 1).

2. Write out Psalm 119:14-16.

3. Look up the following verses and describe what you discover about riches. Carefully consider the contrast between spiritual and earthly wealth. Remember that the purpose of the prayer of this great Psalm is for the Lord to bring us into *His will* for our lives.

    Proverbs 3:13-18

    Matthew 13:44-46

    Luke 12:16-21

    Romans 11:33

Tuesday - continued

4. Write down the six action phrases found in Psalm 119:13-16.

   a. e.g., I have told

   b.

   c.

   d.

   e.

   f.

5. Rewrite these six action phrases in your own words. This time use the entire statement.

   a. e.g., I am always talking about the Word of God.

   b.

   c.

   d.

   e.

   f.

Wednesday

1. Read and meditate on Psalm 119:17-24 (supplemental reading: Psalm 58).

2. Write out Psalm 119:17a.

3. Considering yesterday's study, what kind of *bounty* do you think David desired?

4. Write out Psalm 119:17b.

5. David does not desire to simply live but to live in subjection to God's will. There are multitudes of people who live without any real concern for keeping the word of God. My experience is that life without the Lord is utter hell; even life with little of the Lord's presence is misery. Living with a great sense of God's presence is the abundant life we have been promised. Eternity is simply the endless continuation of the life we led on earth—only without the carnal charms that kept people temporarily entertained. People who go to hell have received exactly what they desired: life without God's rule and without His presence. Scripture offers a terrible picture of this in the tragic story of Cain, who rebelled against the Lord's will and ended up banished from His presence, wandering the world with God's curse upon him. Do you know any unbelievers who really epitomize the reality of this? Describe what it is like to be around them.

Wednesday - *continued*

6. Read the following commentary and explain what you learn about the correlation between our attitude in praying for God's bounty and God's ability to fulfill our request.

He takes pleasure in owning his duty to God, and counts it the joy of his heart to be in the service of his God. Out of his condition he makes a plea, for a servant has some hold upon a master; but in this case the wording of the plea shuts out the idea of legal claim, since he seeks bounty rather than reward. Let my wages be according to thy goodness, and not according to my merit. Reward me according to the largeness of thy liberality, and not according to the scantiness of my service...

David felt that his great needs required a bountiful provision, and that his little desert would never earn such a supply; hence he must throw himself upon God's grace, and look for the great things he needed from the great goodness of the Lord. He begs for a liberality of grace, after the fashion of one who prayed. "O Lord, thou must give me great mercy or no mercy, for little mercy will not serve my turn."[2]

Thursday

1. Read and meditate on Psalm 119:17-24 (supplemental reading: Psalm 24).

2. Write out Psalm 119:18.

3. Look up Ephesians 1:18 and explain the great spiritual truth touched upon by both David and Paul.

4. Pick five statements from the following quote by Charles Spurgeon and explain what you derived from each of them.

> Some men can perceive no wonders in the gospel, but David felt sure that there were glorious things in the law: he had not half the Bible, but he prized it more than some men prize the whole. He felt that God had laid up great bounties in his word, and he begs for power to perceive, appreciate, and enjoy the same. We need not so much that God should give us more benefits, as the ability to see what he has given.
>
> The prayer implies a conscious darkness, a dimness of spiritual vision, a powerlessness to remove that defect, and a full assurance that God can remove it. It shows also that the writer knew that there were vast treasures in the word which he had not yet fully seen, marvels which he had not yet beheld, mysteries which he had scarcely believed. The Scriptures teem with marvels; the Bible is wonder-land; it not only relates miracles, but it is itself a world of wonders. Yet what are these to closed eyes? And what man can open his own eyes, since he is born blind? God himself must reveal revelation to each heart. Scripture needs opening, but not one half so much as our eyes do; the veil is not on the book, but on our hearts. What perfect precepts, what precious promises, what priceless privileges are neglected by us because we wander among them like blind men amongst the beauties of nature, and they are to us as a landscape shrouded in darkness![3]

   a.

   b.

   c.

   d.

   e.

Friday

1. Read and meditate on Psalm 119:17-24 (supplemental reading: Psalm 17).

2. Write out Psalm 119:19, 21.

3. David did not view this world as his true home. Look up the following verses and describe what you learn.

   I Chronicles 29:15

   Psalm 39:12

   Philippians 3:20

   Hebrews 11:9-10

   Hebrews 11:13-16

4. Compare the different Bible translations provided below with your own translation. What fresh concepts are revealed to you in each of these verses?

   a. Psalm 119:9 "How shall a young man cleanse his way? By taking heed and keeping watch [on himself] according to Your word [conforming his life to it]." (AMP)

   b. Psalm 119:19 "My soul is overcome with an incessant longing for your rulings." (JER)

   c. Psalm 119:20 "I am overwhelmed continually with a desire for your laws." (NLT)

Saturday

1. Read and meditate on Psalm 119:9-24 (supplemental reading: Psalm 40).

2. Do you consider your inner life to be morally pure? If not, why not? What do you think you can and should do to purify yourself?

3. Take another look at the six action phrases you examined in Tuesday's homework. Would you say that these phrases more aptly describe your love for the kingdom of God *or* the different appetites you have for the things of this world? Explain your answer and, if you feel that the latter is the case, express in writing your commitment to God to change.

4. Reread the Spurgeon quote in Thursday's homework. Does the Bible truly thrill your soul? If not, Matthew 13:15 might provide a hint as to why that is. Explain what you learn and how it relates to your personal life.

Sunday

ISRAEL'S FIRST KING
I Samuel 8-15

Had it not been for the people of Israel demanding a king, Saul, son of Kish the Benjamite, would be completely unknown to us. His emergence from obscurity in 1050 B.C. came as a direct result of the people's rebellion against theocratic rule. God, rather than giving the Israelites a man after His heart, gave them what they wanted, a king after their own heart. At nearly seven feet tall, rugged and handsome, Saul was the prototypical male. The people instantly adored him.

Saul began his controversial reign modestly, being "little in his own sight." When the Ammonites threatened the Jewish inhabitants of Jabesh-Gilead, he rallied the people from north to south and soundly defeated them. He was hailed as a national hero and became the catalyst to unite as a nation the disjointed clans of Israel. Solomon would later say that a man "is tested by the praise accorded him," and it is highly likely that, as he basked in the adoration of the people, the seeds of Saul's downfall were sown.

The Israelites had already been drifting away from their earlier commitment to Jehovah and once again found themselves facing heathen oppression. The Philistines, the last remnant of the advanced civilization of the Manoans of Crete, had brought with them iron weapons, giving them a deadly advantage over the Jewish people.

Two years after his coronation, Saul summoned an army from across Israel to meet him in Gilgal. Meanwhile, Samuel sent word to him that he would arrive within seven days to offer a special sacrifice to the Lord, thus assuring victory for the Israelites. As Saul waited anxiously, the Philistines began amassing their own mighty army. Pressure mounted. Fearful men began deserting. Finally, the seventh day arrived, but the prophet was still nowhere to be seen.

For the young monarch, this was a divine test: Would he humbly obey, or would he presumptuously disregard the Lord's command in the face of pressure? Saul decided that he would offer the sacrifice himself—something absolutely forbidden in the Torah.

No sooner had he finished than the solemn prophet with the penetrating gaze arrived on the scene. "You have acted foolishly!" he thundered. "The Lord would have established your kingdom over Israel forever. But now your kingdom shall not endure."

As many years passed, the monarch capriciously settled into his reign. In the meantime, the Lord saw something no one else could discern: the Amalekites—a wild, marauding people who lived on the Negev—had crossed a dangerous line spiritually. The cup of their iniquity was now full and running over. The Lord decided He would use His chosen people to execute judgment on this devil-infested nation. This would also afford Saul the opportunity to redeem himself. The orders were crystal clear: Saul was to annihilate the entire nation.

Unfortunately, it seems the Jewish dictator had grown weary of the divine controls on his life and reign. He obeyed the Lord… partially. Everything and everyone was destroyed but the Amalekite king—who would be kept as a personal trophy to be showed off—and some of the animals to appease his greedy soldiers. Then, to further kindle the Lord's wrath, Saul hosted a victory celebration and built a monument *to himself!*

Arriving the next day, Samuel immediately confronted the rebel king. "When you were small in your own sight, were you not made the head of the tribes of Israel?", Samuel asked. (I Samuel 15:17 AMP) A long and prosperous reign awaited him had he remained faithful to the Lord.

Displaying unmitigated brazenness, Saul exaggerated his obedience and minimized his wrongdoing. But the old prophet would have none of it. "To obey is better than sacrifice… For rebellion is as the sin of divination, and insubordination is as iniquity and idolatry. Because you have rejected the word of the Lord, He has also rejected you from being king. (I Samuel 15:22,23)

Saul, who had forgotten that he was appointed as God's delegated authority over the nation of Israel, had become big in his own sight—too big to obey. Now the Lord would send His faithful servant out to find "a man after His own heart." Saul would remain king for years to come, but his days were numbered and his dynasty would eventually come to a bitter end.

WEEK 3: LONGING TO BE KEPT

Monday

1. Read and meditate on Psalm 119:25-32 (supplemental reading: Psalm 6).

2. As previously stated, Psalm 119 was written as a prayer; thus, it cannot be fully comprehended through a purely academic study. This week we will focus on learning how to actually pray-read Scripture. We will examine the prayer of a friend of mine through the next two stanzas. Over the course of some 30 years, he has prayed through Psalm 119 hundreds of times.

    Let's begin with the fourth stanza, which is David's plea for his heart to be conquered by the Lord. Carefully examine this prayer through verses 25-32, comparing each sentence with the corresponding verse. As you go through it, underline five of the phrases from his prayer that are especially meaningful to you. Then, on the next page, explain what you gained from each.

    vs. 25 - Precious Lord, my soul cleaves to the dust of this earthly life. Won't you please give me life according to Your wonderful life-giving word?

    vs. 26 - I have declared my ways, plenty; and You heard me; but teach me now Your statutes. Give me the words of Jesus as the thing I need to learn.

    vs. 27 - Make me to understand the way of Your precepts. As Your precious Son said, "No longer do I call you slaves, for the slave does not know what his master is doing; but I have called you friends, for all things that I have heard from My Father I have made known to you." Lord, make me to understand the way of my friend, Jesus. And then I will surely talk of Your wondrous works.

    vs. 28 - Lord, I am so sick of what I am like. My soul is melting for heaviness, but You will strengthen me, won't You dear Lord, according to Your word?

    vs. 29 - Lord, I am deceptive to the core of my being. Will You please take out of me the way of lying; not just lying but the whole way of it; the whole structure of deceit so that I can't even remember how to lie.

    vs. 30 - I have chosen the way of truth. You know that, dear God. I have accepted Jesus as my Savior. Please get Your truth into me. Your judgments I have laid before me. You have judged my sin and I have agreed with You.

    vs. 31 - I have stuck unto Your testimonies. I'm a Christian. I believe in Jesus. Please, Lord, don't let me be a shame to You; because if You don't change me I will be a shame and a reproach to You.

    vs. 32 - Lord, I promise that I will run the way of thy commandments, when You enlarge my heart. I won't be able to help it. Whatever You command me to do, I will run to do it.

Monday - continued

a.

b.

c.

d.

e.

Tuesday

1. Read and meditate on Psalm 119:25-32 (supplemental reading: Psalm 13).

2. Rewrite each verse of Psalm 119:25-32 in your own words, making it a personal appeal for the Lord to conquer *your* heart. As you do this, be sure to include specific references to the areas of your heart and life that remain unconquered.

   Psalm 119:25

   Psalm 119:26

   Psalm 119:27

   Psalm 119:28

   Psalm 119:29

Tuesday - *continued*

Psalm 119:30

Psalm 119:31

Psalm 119:32

Wednesday

1. Read and meditate on Psalm 119:33-40 (supplemental reading: Psalm 20).

2. Today we will turn our attention to the fifth stanza (Psalm 119:33-40), which is David's plea to be kept by the Lord. We will again look to my friend's prayer as a guide to learning how to pray-read through Scripture. Follow the same exercise you did on Monday: underline five of the phrases from his prayer that are especially meaningful to you. Then explain what you gained from each.

    vs. 33 - Teach me, O LORD, the way of Your statutes. Don't let me think of them in a wrong light. Teach me the way of Your statutes and I will keep it all the way to the end. I won't backslide.

    vs. 34 - Give me understanding, and I will keep Your law. If You will open my understanding, I will keep it. Yes, I will observe it with my whole heart.

    vs. 35 - So please, make me to go in the path of Your commandments, Lord. Even when I'm crying that I don't want to go, make me go anyway! Even if I whine and complain, just make me do the right thing. I'll get it eventually. Because that is what I really want. That's the delight of my heart.

    vs. 36 - Incline my heart unto Your testimonies, Lord. All my inclinations are to have something for SELF. Get the momentum going in the right direction; and not to covetousness. I have had enough of it. Your Word says, "What fruit did you have in those things, when you were yielding your members as instruments of unrighteousness unto sin?" Lord, I know the answer: I had no fruit. It was awful. Tip me the other way so I want to do what's right.

    vs. 37 - Turn away mine eyes from beholding vanity. Don't let me look at what the devil puts in front of my eyes. Pull my eyes away from it, Lord. Give me life in Your way.

    vs. 38 - Establish Your word unto me. Make it rock-solid in me. I am devoted to ever being in awe of Your mercy to me through Jesus Christ and His death.

    vs. 39 - Turn away my reproach which I am afraid of, because Your judgments are so good. Separate the evil from the good in me.

    vs. 40 - Lord, You know how I have longed after Your precepts. Now, please give me life after Your righteousness.

    a.

Wednesday - *continued*

b.

c.

d.

e.

Thursday

1. Read and meditate on Psalm 119:33-40 (supplemental reading: Psalm 21).

2. Rewrite each verse of Psalm 119:33-40 in your own words, making it a personal appeal for the Lord to keep you. As you do this, make sure to mention those areas of vulnerability where you desire to be kept.

    Psalm 119:33

    Psalm 119:34

    Psalm 119:35

    Psalm 119:36

    Psalm 119:37

    Psalm 119:38

    Psalm 119:39

    Psalm 119:40

Friday

1. Read and meditate on Psalm 119:33-40 (supplemental reading: Psalm 33).

2. Write out Psalm 119:34.

3. Psalm 119:34 uses two different words with similar meanings: *observe* (Heb. *shâmar*) and *keep* (Heb. *nâtsar*). For the purposes of our study, let's take a moment to look at the first of these two words. Look up *shâmar*$_{8104}$ in a Bible dictionary and explain what you learn.

4. Read Psalm 121 (provided below) and explain what you learn about the Lord's involvement in your life.

    "I will lift up my eyes to the mountains; from where shall my help come? My help comes from the LORD, Who made heaven and earth. He will not allow your foot to slip; He who keeps (*shâmar*) you will not slumber. Behold, He who keeps (*shâmar*) Israel will neither slumber nor sleep. The LORD is your keeper (*shâmar*); the LORD is your shade on your right hand. The sun will not smite you by day, nor the moon by night. The LORD will protect (*shâmar*) you from all evil; He will keep (*shâmar*) your soul. The LORD will guard (*shâmar*) your going out and your coming in from this time forth and forever."

Friday - *continued*

5. Compare the different Bible translations provided below for the following verses. What fresh concepts are revealed to you in each of these translations?

a. Psalm 119:26:
    "I have described my plight to You, and You have answered me; teach me Your statutes." (HAR)

    "I admitted my behaviour, you answered me, now teach me your statutes." (JER)

    "I put the record of my ways before you, and you gave me an answer: O give me knowledge of your rules." (BAS)

b. Psalm 119:37:
    "Turn me away from wanting any other plan than yours. Revive my heart toward you." (LIV)

    "Avert my eyes from unreality; uphold me in Your true principles." (HAR)

    "Turn away my eyes from beholding vanity (idols and idolatry); and restore me to vigorous life and health in Your ways." (AMP)

Saturday

1. Read and meditate on Psalm 119:25-40 (supplemental reading: Psalm 23).

2. David not only understood that the Lord alone could transform his heart, but also that he had to be faithful to do his part. List the five "I" statements of his in verses 27 and 30-32.

    a.

    b.

    c.

    d.

    e.

3. Now go back over these five statements and rate yourself on a scale of one to ten (10 meaning *constantly*; 1 meaning *never*) according to the frequency you actually do what is expressed. Be brutally honest.

    a.

    b.

    c.

    d.

    e.

4. In Psalm 119:33-39, each request begins with an action which the Psalmist desires the Lord to perform for him. Write down in short form what he wants in each verse.

    a. Psalm 119:33 e.g., teach me the way

    b. Psalm 119:34

    c. Psalm 119:35

Saturday - *continued*

    d. Psalm 119:36

    e. Psalm 119:37

    f. Psalm 119:38

    g. Psalm 119:39

5.   I believe that if a person sincerely wants to be kept by the Lord, He will keep him. However, if he or she does not want to be kept (or simply doesn't care), God will let that person have his or her own way. Based on your own experience, do you agree with these statements? Explain your answer.

DAVID'S BOYHOOD
I Samuel 16

Sunday

Saul's reign was barely two years old when he was rejected by the Lord for disobedience. It was then that Samuel ominously declared, "The Lord has sought out for Himself a man after His own heart…" (I Samuel 13:14)

David was the youngest of Jesse's eight sons. As such, on him eventually fell the ignoble task of caring for the family's flock of sheep in the Judean wilds. Life in the wilderness was one of the most undesirable things that could be required of a man. While the rest of the family enjoyed hot meals, warm beds and joyous times of fellowship, the shepherd was forced to endure the frigid nights and scorching days of the Negev, tedious hours of boredom, and constant threat of danger from wild animals or marauding gangs of heathens.

The wilderness—where the character of godly men is forged—would be home for the ruddy son of Jesse for much of his younger years. While most of us have a difficult time imagining daily life without modern conveniences and titillating entertainment, David spent weeks at a time in desert isolation. With no television, Internet, or video games to distract him, the earnest adolescent spent many hours sitting in the presence of God. It's evident from his early writings, such as Psalm 23, that he was already "rich toward God."

Following Samuel's nerve-wracking encounter with the rebel king after the Amalekite affair, we are told that "Samuel grieved over Saul." This mourning period probably lasted a few weeks until, finally, the Lord admonished the prophet: "How long will you grieve over Saul… ? Fill your horn with oil and go; I will send you to Jesse the Bethlehemite, for I have selected a king for Myself among his sons." (I Samuel 16:1)

The word *selected* (Heb. *râ'âh*) is a verb usually translated "to see." Thus, the literal interpretation of this verse would read: "…for I have seen a king for Myself…" This is reaffirmed a few verses later where we find the Lord chiding Samuel for looking upon the outward appearance, while "the Lord *looks* at the heart." This Jehovah Rapha (the God who sees) is "He who searches the minds and hearts." (Revelation 2:23) When

He "sought a man after His own heart," it could be said that He went from man to man, looking at their hearts, stopping only when He had found the right one in the sheepfolds of Bethlehem.

Samuel then anointed the astonished teenager, apparently effecting the transference of the Holy Spirit from one person to another, for we are told, "Now the Spirit of the Lord departed from Saul, and an evil spirit from the Lord terrorized him." (I Samuel 16:14) And apparently at the same time, "…the Spirit of Jehovah came mightily upon David from that day forward." (I Samuel 16:13)

Unquestionably, God had His mighty hand on David's life. Having already given the young man a rich spiritual education in the wilderness, the Lord now purposed to add two important elements. The first lesson would come in the tent of the king. In the same way that He had prepared Moses in Pharaoh's palace, God now arranged for David to spend time with the king of Israel.

Saul longed for relief from the relentless demon that tormented him. It just so happened that one of his men came in contact with David and walked away extremely impressed, calling him "a skillful musician, a mighty man of valor, a warrior, one prudent in speech, and a handsome man; and the Lord is with him." (I Samuel 16:18) From that time on, David spent time in the king's court, playing his harp, worshiping Jehovah and, in so doing, driving off the devil that plagued Saul.

The second episode that was instrumental in preparing David for the great call upon his life was the valuable time he spent with Samuel. It seems clear that the old prophet invited the teenager to join him in his "school of the prophets." "Samuel gave unto David that which Saul had not received — long and careful training; and David profited by it, and at Naioth in Ramah perfected his skill, not only in reading and writing, but in poetry and music. Samuel carefully educated him in the law of God, and led his mind onward to all that was good. It was Samuel's last and crowning work."[1]

This special training would be crucial for the great challenges that awaited David.

WEEK 4: DAVID'S LOVE—GOD'S WORD

Monday

1. Read and meditate on Psalm 119:41-48 (supplemental reading: Psalm 136).

2. Write out Psalm 119:41.

3. Read the following passage about *lovingkindness* and explain what you learn.

> Mercy is living out the love of God. The Old Testament Hebrew word translated mercy in the King James Bible is *hhesed*. It is translated as "lovingkindness" in the NASB and "unfailing love" in the NIV. *Hhesed* primarily refers to the supply system God established on this earth to meet needs: physical, emotional, and spiritual. As one brother stated:
>
> "Mercy is the radiation of love. Just as there is but one sun in our skies and yet endless rays from our sun, so there are ENDLESS MERCIES from the holy fire of divine love, a love which can never be extinguished... .
>
> If we are hungry, mercy is food. If we are thirsty, mercy is water. If we are cold, mercy is warmth and heat and shelter and clothing. If we are discouraged, mercy is encouragement and strength. If we are rebellious, mercy is repentance. If we are guilty (and repent), mercy is pardon. If we are defeated, mercy is victory."[1]

Monday - *continued*

4. Explain why you think David longed for God's lovingkindnesses to come to him.

5. Explain why David equated salvation with God's lovingkindness.

6. Read the account of Jesus with the Pharisees found in Matthew 9:11-13. Verse 13 is a quotation from the book of Hosea where this word *hhesed* is used. Jesus realized that the Pharisees were in great trouble spiritually. This is one of the few times He actually told them to do something. Explain what you think might have happened in the life of a Pharisee who sincerely followed His instructions.

Tuesday

1. Read and meditate on Psalm 119:41-48 (supplemental reading: Psalm 29).

2. Write out Psalm 119:42.

3. In Hebrews 3, the tragic story of the failure of the Israelites in the wilderness is hauntingly recounted. How different was David's life! Read Hebrews 3:1-4:2 and answer the following questions.

   a. Compare Psalm 119:42b with Hebrews 4:1-2. Explain the main difference between David's relationship to God and that of his ancestors.

   b. Compare Psalm 119:44 with Hebrews 3:17-18. Describe the difference between David's life and that of his ancestors.

   c. According to Hebrews 3:19, what was the ultimate reason for the failure of the Israelites in the wilderness?

4. Not only did David say that he trusted God's word, but twice in this stanza he said that he loved it. Examine each of the following phrases and briefly describe in your own words how he displayed that love through his actions.

   a. 119:43b

   b. 119:45b

   c. 119:46a

   d. 119:47a

   e. 119:48a

   f. 119:48b

Wednesday

1. Read and meditate on Psalm 119:41-48 (supplemental reading: Psalm 103).

2. In Psalm 119:44, we find the same Hebrew word *shâmar* that we looked at last Friday. In the NASB, it is translated as *observe* in verse 34 and *keep* in verse 44. Rewrite Psalm 119:44-45 in your own words, keeping in mind what you learned about this important concept.

3. What two things, according to verses 44 and 45, accounted for David's liberty?

   a.   b.

4. Can you see any difference between David's understanding of liberty and the popular understanding of liberty in our culture? Explain your answer.

5. In Psalm 119:42-48, the pronoun "I" is used 12 times. List the accompanying noun and verb with each instance:

		Verb	Noun			Verb	Noun
a.	42a e.g.	will have	answer	g.	46a		
b.	42b			h.	47a		
c.	43b			i.	47b		
d.	44a			j.	48a		
e.	45a			k.	48b		
f.	45b						

6. Read I John 3:18 and explain what the list above reveals about David's love for God's Word.

Thursday

1. Read and meditate on Psalm 119:49-56 (supplemental reading: Psalm 2).

2. Write out the following phrases.

    a. Psalm 119:44a

    b. Psalm 119:51b

    c. Psalm 119:53

    d. Psalm 119:55b

3. Read the following excerpt and explain what you learn.

    The concept of law (Gk., *nomos*) goes beyond the commandments of God given in the Pentateuch. In fact, every culture, no matter how primitive (or how rebellious to God's prescribed law), has a set of customs which establish what is to be considered right and wrong for that particular society. The primary meaning of *nomos* is "what is proper," and the opposite of *nomos* is *anomos,* which means to live without law or to adopt an attitude of lawlessness. According to Vine's Expository Dictionary, *anomos* means more than committing an unlawful act; it means "flagrant defiance of the known will of God." Anyone who lives in self-will is *anomos*—lawless... .

    This attitude of rebellion has spilled over into the lives of believers. Had the spirit of this world blatantly tried to thrust its mentality on the Church, the attempt would have failed. Our leaders would have set aside their differences and become unified in their opposition to it. However, Satan is much too crafty for such a frontal assault. Rather, he has beguiled the Church by a subtle, slow and *mysterious* attack on our standards of godliness. What the spirit of Antichrist could never have done overtly, it has accomplished by stealth.

    Little by little, one corruption after another has been introduced into the framework and corporate mentality of American Christianity to the point where the Church has lost its moorings. The changes in the last thirty years have lowered standards for today's ministers below the standards of yesterday's layperson! Anyone whose conscience urges him to abstain from worldliness is mocked and labeled a fanatic. And the definition of "worldliness" is so watered down that the worldliness I'm talking about involves activities which would have shocked believers of a generation ago!

    The daily saturation of shocking news and illicit behavior via television, newspapers, magazines, and the Internet has left Christians spiritually and emotionally numb. It's hard to be affected by anything. Images of the wicked behavior of lawless people fill our minds, stain our souls and influence our hearts. We've become so corrupted that we no longer even feel the need for holiness! It is understandable for the world to think a zealous believer is strange, but for the Church to view a consecrated saint with suspicion, derision, and even contempt shows how corporately backslidden Christendom truly is.[2]

Thursday - *continued*

4. Look up the following verses and explain what you learn about *lawlessness*.

   Matthew 7:21-23

   Matthew 13:41-42

   Matthew 23:28

   Matthew 24:12

   Romans 6:19

   II Corinthians 6:14

   II Thessalonians 2:3, 7

   I John 3:4

Friday

1. Read and meditate on Psalm 119:49-56 (supplemental reading: Psalm 31).

2. Write out Psalm 119:52, 55.

3. David has appealed to God's memory in verse 49, but he also describes his own remembrances. Look up the following verses and explain what you learn about *remembering*.

   Numbers 11:4-6

   Judges 8:34

   I Chronicles 16:12

   Luke 17:32

   John 15:20

   Acts 20:35

   Revelation 2:5:

Friday - continued

4. Pick one of the passages listed on the previous page that could be applicable to you at some point in your life. Explain how your memory was a tool to lead you to do something positive or negative.

5. Compare the different Bible translations provided below with your own translation. What fresh concepts are revealed to you in each of these verses?

   a. Psalm 119:43 "Do not snatch your word of truth from me, for my only hope is in your laws." (NLT)

   b. Psalm 119:44-45 "I will keep Your law continually, forever and ever [hearing, receiving, loving, and obeying it]. And I will walk at liberty and at ease, for I have sought and inquired for [and desperately required] Your precepts." (AMP)

   c. Psalm 119:47 "How I love your laws! How I enjoy your commands!" (LIV)

   d. Psalm 119:49 "Don't forget your promise to me, your servant. I depend on it." (CEV)

Saturday

1. Read and meditate on Psalm 119:41-56 (supplemental reading: Psalm 118).

2. Reread the passage about lovingkindness in Monday's homework. Mention briefly ten instances in your life where God has met your needs in some way.

    a.

    b.

    c.

    d.

    e.

    f.

    g.

    h.

    i.

    j.

3. Reread the passage from *Intoxicated with Babylon* provided in Thursday's homework. Examine your own life and explain how the prevailing atmosphere of lawlessness affects your walk with God.

CAMP FIGHTERS
I Samuel 17

Sunday

David spent the next few years shuffling between multiple locales—Bethlehem with his father, Gibeah with King Saul and Ramah with Samuel. All three locations offered their own distinct forms of training for the teenager. The time David spent in the king's court provided a private education that must have thrilled him. When released from his duties there, David had the privilege of being personally tutored by one of the spiritual giants of all time. If all this was heady stuff for the teen, he was quickly brought down to earth at home with his family.

Meanwhile, trouble was brewing for the nation of Israel. The Philistines, seemingly incognizant of the profound trouncing they received some 15 years before, decided it was time to reestablish their old dominance over their hated Semitic neighbors.

They gathered about 15 miles west of Bethlehem, in an obscure but aptly named rural location called Ephes-dammim—"Boundaries of Blood." Saul and his army assembled on one hilltop while the Philistines amassed their forces on an opposing knoll. Between them lay the expansive Valley of Elah, which gently sloped downward, until, at the bottom, it abruptly dropped into a narrow ravine.

A stalemate ensued as both armies refused to venture out from their impregnable positions. In those days, one way to resolve such an impasse was for each militia to put forth their champion—the toughest fighter they had in their ranks—for a fight to the death.

The Philistine army, though depleted and lacking the necessary strength to overcome the stronger Jewish military, did possess a secret weapon that gave them a distinct advantage. Within their ranks were a few survivors of the ancient race of Anakim. Among them was Goliath who, at nine feet tall, was the kind of camp fighter that could bolster the weakest army. The giant with the murderous spirit had spilled much blood during his lifetime. Extremely arrogant, he seemed to relish such opportunities to slaughter other men.

Meanwhile, David arrived with food for his brothers, just in time to hear the vulgar taunts of the giant, challenging the Israelites to produce their own champion to rival him. At the sound of Goliath's booming voice, the trembling Jews retreated back to the security of their hilltop stronghold.

Undoubtedly, David also feared this monster, but with the Holy Spirit resting upon him, and a righteous anger burning within him he refused to give in to fear. He immediately went to the old king and offered to fight Goliath. "You are but a youth," Saul argued. But David had already experienced the power of God upon his body when he encountered a lion and a bear out in the wilderness. He would not be talked out of it.

Down the sloping hillside the young man went. Once he stepped out of the Israelite camp, there was no turning back. He was all alone, with several thousand eyes watching his every move. It was customary for each combatant to make a little speech of disdainment toward the other before the fight actually began. Goliath took the opportunity to mock David, his God and his people. David responded with a boldness borne out of humble faith in the Lord. Though the youthful Israelite was probably quite adept at using a sling, his confidence did not rest upon any abilities he might have had, but in the Living God.

David scampered down into the ravine, picked up a few stones, and ascended the other side. "Then came the terrible moment, and both armies held their breath for a time. David made the attack. Nimbly he ran forward to be within shot. Goliath had opened the visor of his helmet to look at the foe whom he despised, and to shout defiance. Thus was his forehead exposed. David's quick eye saw the advantage; he slipped a pebble into the sling, and let it fly. A sharp whistle in the air, and the stone sunk into the giant's haughty brow. "He fell on his face to the earth. How the men of Israel shouted as they heard the clang of his heavy armour on the ground, and saw their young champion cut off the boaster's head with his own sword!"[3]

It was a tremendous victory for the Israelites, who pursued the fleeing Philistines all the way back to Ekron. In a matter of moments, this meek young shepherd had become a triumphant national hero.

WEEK 5: BACK ON TRACK

Monday

1. Read and meditate on Psalm 119:57-64 (supplemental reading: Psalm 16).

2. Write out Psalm 119:57.

3. It could be said that Psalm 16 is a commentary on this verse. Please turn to this Psalm and answer the following questions.

    a. What do you think David meant when he said in Psalm 16:2, "I have no good besides You."?

    b. Read the following quote from Albert Barnes. Do you think this could be an appropriate commentary on Psalm 119:57? Explain your answer.

    > "My good is nowhere except in thee; I have no source of good of any kind— happiness, hope, life, safety, salvation—but in thee.… ." In other words, he found in Yahweh all that is implied in the idea of an object of worship—all that is properly expressed by the notion of a God. He renounced all other gods, and found his happiness—his all—in Yahweh.[1]

    c. How does this kind of life expressed by David contrast with what he describes in Psalm 16:4a?

Monday - continued

d. Read Psalm 16:5-6. This refers primarily to the land survey done when a man dies and his property must be divided amongst his heirs. A biblical picture of this can be seen in Joshua 14 where faithful Caleb is allotted a choice piece of the Promised Land as an inheritance. How do you think this applies to a New Testament believer?

e. In Psalm 16:9, David refers to gladness, rejoicing and a sense of security. Now read 16:8 and explain why he had such inward joy.

f. Rewrite Psalm 16:11 in your own words.

Tuesday

1. Read and meditate on Psalm 119:57-64 (supplemental reading: Psalm 61).

2. Write out Psalm 119:59-60.

3. These two verses are a wonderful picture of real repentance. What do you think David was referring to when he said, "I considered my ways"?

4. Do you see apathy or urgency being expressed in verse 60? Explain your answer.

5. Can you think of any biblical characters who actually did what David refers to here? If so, tell the story in light of these two verses. If you cannot think of anyone, please refer to 5a in the Appendix (page 138) for some examples.

6. Can you think of any biblical characters who refused to consider their ways and repent? If so, tell the story in light of these two verses. If you cannot think of anyone, please refer to 5b in the Appendix (page 138) for some examples.

1. Read and meditate on Psalm 119:57-64 (supplemental reading: Psalm 5).

2. Write out Psalm 119:62-63.

3. Read the following commentary and explain what you learn.

> The Hebrew here means, literally, "the half," or "halving of the night," the night considered as divided into two equal portions. The idea is, that his mind was so full of the subject that he would take this unusual time to give vent to his feelings. The mind may be so full of love to the law—the word—of God, that nothing will satisfy it but such unusual acts of devotion.[2]

4. David understood a very important spiritual fact: it is vital to make a solid connection with God every day and this best happens in the solitude of the night or early morning. Look up the following verses and describe what you learn about David's prayer life.

Psalm 4:4

Psalm 5:1-3

Wednesday - continued

Psalm 59:16

Psalm 63:6

5. Would you say that David fit his devotional life into his busy life as he could, or would you say that it took precedence over other important areas of his daily life? Explain your answer.

6. What do you think David had in common with those who feared God?

7. Read Matthew 12:46-50 and explain what you think Jesus meant by His statement.

Thursday

1. Read and meditate on Psalm 119:65-72 (supplemental reading: Psalm 9).

2. Write out Psalm 119:67 and 71.

3. Compare these two verses with what David said in Psalm 119:65 and 68. Do you think he is contradicting himself? How could he use such terms to refer to a God who allowed affliction to enter his life? Explain your answer.

4. Please read Hebrews 12:4-11 and list five benefits to God's discipline.

    a.

    b.

    c.

    d.

    e.

Thursday - *continued*

5. Please look up the following verses in the book of Proverbs and briefly describe in your own words the positive or negative consequence of one's reaction to discipline.

POSITIVE	NEGATIVE
10:17a	
10:17b	
12:1a	
12:1b	
13:18a	
13:18b	
15:10a	
15:10b	
29:1	

Friday

1. Read and meditate on Psalm 119:65-72 (supplemental reading: Psalm 84).

2. Write out Psalm 119:68.

3. Look up the following verses and describe what you learn from each about *goodness*.

   Psalm 16:2

   Psalm 25:8

   Psalm 34:8

   Psalm 84:11

   Psalm 103:5

   Psalm 107:1, 9

4. Compare the different Bible translations provided below for the following verses. What fresh concepts are revealed to you in each of these translations?

   a. Psalm 119:57
   "Thou, Lord, art all I have; I have promised to keep thy word." (NEB)

   "LORD, you are mine! I promise to obey your words!" (NLT)

Friday - continued

"You are all I want, O LORD; I promise to obey your laws." (GNB)

b. Psalm 119:67
"In earlier days I had to suffer, I used to stray, but now I remember your promise." (JER)

"I used to wander off until you punished me; now I closely follow all you say." (LIV)

"Before I was afflicted I went astray, but now Your word do I keep [hearing, receiving, loving, and obeying it]." (AMP)

c. Psalm 119:71
"When you corrected me, it did me good because it taught me to study your laws." (CEV)

"The punishment you gave me was the best thing that could have happened to me, for it taught me to pay attention to your laws." (LIV)

"My punishment was good for me, because it made me learn your commands." (GNB)

Saturday

1. Read and meditate on Psalm 119:57-72 (supplemental reading: Psalm 18).

2. Compare what is expressed in Psalm 16:2 with 16:4a. Examine the interests you give yourself to in your daily life—the things that you allow to crowd in on your devotion to God. Can you see how those idols—as entertaining as they are to the flesh—drain and empty you spiritually? Can you see how over time that they will bring upon your life the sorrow of an empty soul? Explain your answers.

3. Verses 59 and 60 describe a man who is continually reviewing his life to see if he is remaining faithful to the Lord or if he has wandered astray. The Word of God establishes this path. Do you regularly examine your heart and daily life to see how you are doing? If not, why not? Explain your answers.

4. Considering the effects the world, the flesh and the devil have on your life, explain why you feel that repentance should be a regular feature of your daily life.

Saturday - continued

5. How solid would you consider your prayer life to be? If it isn't what you think it should be, what can you do to improve it?

6. Look at verses 67 and 71 in the different Bible translations in yesterday's homework. Would these statements be representative of your life as well? Explain your answer.

Sunday

THE RISE AND FALL OF YOUNG DAVID
I Samuel 18

In the years following the frowning prophet's stinging rebuke, a gloomy pall had settled over King Saul's reign. However, with the great victory at Elah, this now seemed to dissipate and an unexpected gleam of light began to break forth upon the consciousness of the melancholy king. With the threat of the Philistines now a thing of the past, and with champions like David and Jonathan supporting him, the future suddenly looked bright and prosperous.

For Jonathan, 40-year-old prince of Israel, there also flashed great hope. He hadn't seen joy on his father's face in many years. He also now had a new friend—someone else who understood what it meant to believe God for victory. Never mind that David was much younger; the two of them shared a common faith and a deep and lasting friendship.

The people of Israel were ecstatically relieved. They well remembered the long years of cruel oppression by the Philistines. But now all their fears were allayed! Israel had a champion that would make any nation proud. From Dan to Beersheba, the name of David was uttered with gratitude and admiration.

As for David himself, his life would never again be the same. The quiet solitude and relative obscurity in the fields of Bethlehem was forever gone, replaced in one day by the clamorous demands of national prominence. "One can hardly imagine a course of events more likely to turn a young man's head and make him giddy with elation than the rapid promotion of the youthful David… David leaped at a bound into honour and fame, but for that very reason he found himself at the beginning of his troubles. Well that, before those troubles began to press him, he knew the Lord as his refuge."[3]

Saul immediately appointed David as a captain in his army. During the ensuing months and years, David amassed an impressive number of victories. "So his name was highly esteemed." (I Samuel 18:30b) It is interesting to note some of the synonyms for the Hebraic word for esteemed (*yaqar*): precious, valuable, costly, rare, and splendid. These terms aptly describe the people of Israel's great admiration for this young warrior.

However, David's characteristic humility soon manifested itself. When Saul's servants approached him about the possibility of marrying the king's daughter, David exclaimed, "Is it trivial in your sight to become the king's son-in-law, since I am a poor man and lightly esteemed?" (I Samuel 18:18) Note the vast disparity between David's self-perception and others' admiration for him. Be that as it may, a song had begun to ring loudly throughout the land: "Saul has slain his thousands, and David his ten thousands." (I Samuel 18:7)

Unbeknownst to the humble soldier, those words were echoing in the ears of a grim king. Over and over they sounded in his mind, further exacerbated by a tormenting demon. At first, Saul was thrilled about his new champion, but as time passed, excitement gave way to suspicion. In truth, Saul could not tolerate anyone receiving more praise than himself.

The more heroic deeds David performed to please his king and advance the interests of his nation, the angrier and more miserable the old monarch became. Had Saul been willing to humble himself, this godly young man might have helped him make amends with the Lord and rectify his past mistakes. But Saul, ever blinded by self-ambition, could only see a threat to his position. Day after day, the poison of envy ate away at his soul. As David's insightful son would later write, "Wrath is fierce and anger is a flood, but who can stand before jealousy?" (Proverbs 27:4)

Then, just when everything looked so promising for young David, the Lord inexplicably allowed an already tense situation to worsen. "Now it came about on the next day that an evil spirit from God came mightily upon Saul, and he raved in the midst of the house, while David was playing the harp with his hand, as usual; and a spear was in Saul's hand. And Saul hurled the spear for he thought, 'I will pin David to the wall.' But David escaped from his presence twice." (I Samuel 18:11)

Thus began the long and painful decline of an innocent young man who wanted only to serve his king.

WEEK 6: SPIRITUAL LONGINGS

Monday

1. Read and meditate on Psalm 119:73-80 (supplemental reading: Psalm 139).

2. Write out Psalm 119:73.

3. Look up the following verses and describe what you learn about the inward man.

    Psalm 33:15

    Psalm 139:13-14

    Zechariah 12:1

    Luke 11:39-40

Monday - continued

Ephesians 2:10

4. In light of these verses, what do you think David was asking for in Psalm 119:73?

5. The inward life of a man is of extreme importance to the Lord. Read the following extract from my book, *At the Altar of Sexual Idolatry*, and explain what you learn.

> We all have an inside world that is made up of the different parts of our inner man: the heart, soul, mind, spirit, will, intellect and emotions. It is the life that goes on inside of us: our thoughts, feelings, attitudes, sentiments and opinions. This is where dreams are born and failures grieved, the place where intricate processes are put into motion and life's decisions are contemplated. Here we also find the conflicting emotions of love and hate, like and dislike, attraction and repulsion. Our inside world is where we live our daily existence. Some people are considered "open" because they are not afraid to show their thoughts and feelings with other people. Others are thought to be "closed," feeling anxious when people become too intimate. Regardless of how willing a person is to talk about his feelings, the truth is, he will never completely allow another to intimately know the deepest part of his inner man. This is an extremely private place, an inner sanctum — a holy of holies, so to speak.
>
> The outward life stands in contrast to the inside world. This is how we speak and act in front of other people. We all have an image which we attempt to maintain — a way in which we want other people to view us. One person might want to be seen as someone who is intellectual and cultured. Another might want to portray himself as being tough, while yet another will want to be seen as sweet. The impressions we wish to project are woven into everything we say and do in the presence of other people.[1]

Tuesday

1. Read and meditate on Psalm 119:73-80 (supplemental reading: Psalm 22).

2. Rewrite Psalm 119:73-80, in your own words, as a personal prayer to the Lord.

    Psalm 119:73

    Psalm 119:74

    Psalm 119:75

    Psalm 119:76

    Psalm 119:77

    Psalm 119:78

    Psalm 119:79

    Psalm 119:80

Wednesday

1. Read and meditate on Psalm 119:73-80 (supplemental reading: Psalm 27).

2. Rewrite Psalm 119:75 in your own words.

3. Look up the following instances of the Lord executing His justice upon the wicked and explain what, if any, good you see coming out of it for others. (Hint: Consider how it affected those who witnessed it or those who remained in the area afterward.)

    Genesis 18:20; 19:24-25

    Exodus 14:21-31

    I Samuel 11:5-11

4. The book of Revelation is the heavenly account of God bringing the earth under subjection to His Son. Explain what you think life will be like on this earth when evil has been purged from it.

Wednesday - *continued*

5. The Lord also brings judgment upon His own people. Take a brief look at the stories mentioned below and explain what you learn.

    Leviticus 10:1-3

    Psalm 78:34-35

    Acts 5:8-13

6. The purpose of God's judgment is to separate evil from good. This will certainly be the case at the end of the age, but it is also true within the lives of believers. The Lord constantly works in their lives to purge sin (through judgment) and mold godly character within them (often through affliction). Considering this, explain what you feel David meant in Psalm 119:75.

Thursday

1. Read and meditate on Psalm 119:81-88 (supplemental reading: Psalm 56).

2. Rewrite Psalm 119:81-88 in your own words, making it a personal prayer to the Lord.

Psalm 119:81

Psalm 119:82

Psalm 119:83

Psalm 119:84

Psalm 119:85

Psalm 119:86

Psalm 119:87

Psalm 119:88

Friday

1. Read and meditate on Psalm 119:81-88 (supplemental reading: Psalm 63).

2. Write out Psalm 119:81-83.

3. These verses provide deeper insight into what David touched upon in Psalm 119:74b. Look at what he expresses in these two verses:

   81a.   My soul languishes…
   81b.   I wait…
   82a.   My eyes fail with longing…
   82b.   When?
   83a.   I have become like a wineskin in the smoke…

   These terms and phrases describe something every mature believer has experienced at some point or another. The Lord allows His children to go through periods of darkness; times when they don't understand; seasons of apparently unanswered prayers; trials that never seem to end. The overall intent is to deepen a person's faith in God. Read I Peter 1:6-9 and answer the following questions.

   a. What does I Peter 1:7 say about the value of a person's faith?

   b. What three words does Peter employ to describe the result of that faith?

   c. In verse 8, Peter mentions twice that believers don't see the Lord. In spite of that, what two things does he say believers do?

   d. What is the outcome?

Friday - continued

4. Now take a quick look at James 1:2-3 and describe how it relates to what is being expressed in these verses.

5. Compare the different Bible translations provided below for Psalm 119:81-83. What fresh concepts are revealed to you in each of these translations?

    a. "My soul is wasted with desire for your salvation: but I have hope in your word. My eyes are full of weariness with searching for your word, saying, When will you give me comfort? For I have become like a wine-skin black with smoke; but I still keep the memory of your rules." (BBE)

    b. "My soul languishes and grows faint for Your salvation, but I hope in Your word. My eyes fail, watching for [the fulfillment of] Your promise. I say, When will You comfort me? For I have become like a bottle [a wineskin blackened and shriveled] in the smoke [in which it hangs], yet do I not forget Your statutes." (AMP)

Saturday

1. Read and meditate on Psalm 119:73-88 (supplemental reading: Psalm 59).

2. Please reread the passage from *At the Altar of Sexual Idolatry* provided in Monday's homework. Examine your daily life. What false image of yourself do you attempt to convey to those around you? Can you see how you naturally attempt to present yourself in the most positive light? Can you see how this practice is only one step away from hypocrisy? Explain your answers.

3. The Lord knows how to perfectly balance His dealings with us. I once wrote, "To properly work in a man's life, the Lord takes extensive care over everything He does. Too much scolding can crush a man's spirit. Likewise, excessive leniency could allow him to wander off into unspeakable perils."[2] Can you think of how He has used both positive and negative means to help you to mature? Give an example of each.

4. Have you ever experienced a period of real spiritual dryness? Describe what it felt like and how you knew you had come out of it.

SAUL'S MAD OBSESSION
I Samuel 19-21

Sunday

The watershed moment in Saul's life occurred two years into his reign when he put himself in the place of priest before the great Jehovah. Had he repented following Samuel's confrontation, the outcome of his life could have been much different—but Saul refused to repent. For the next 20 years, he became increasingly entrenched in bitter pride and hardened toward God. Having grieved the Holy Spirit, he was eventually left to the merciless whims of a tormenting devil.

By the time the sweet Psalmist of Bethlehem entered Saul's life, he was already slipping out of the realm of sanity. Self had become enormous in his inside world. Pride, like a snarling watchdog, viciously guarded his personal interests. Anyone who seemed like a threat was dealt with summarily.

As David's popularity grew, so did Saul's apprehension. The verbs employed in I Samuel 18 reveal his tumultuous inner life: anger (vs. 8), suspicion (vs. 9), fear (vs. 12) and finally, dread (vs. 15). These unfettered, self-centered emotions eventually led him to plot David's death. His sinister plan was to entice the young upstart with the prospect of marrying his daughter Michal, demanding the foreskins of a hundred Philistines as the purchase price for her hand. We are given a glimpse into Saul's dark inner world in verse 17: "Saul thought, 'My hand shall not be against him, but let the hand of the Philistines be against him.'"

In his madness, the deranged king had failed to consider the incontrovertible fact that God was with David. It wasn't long before the young warrior returned successfully from his expedition with a bloody pouch full of foreskins. Such was David's love and loyalty to the king that he even killed twice the required number.

His plot having failed, Saul's seething hatred of his imagined rival was unmasked as he ordered Jonathan to kill David. Jonathan reasoned with his father, who temporarily came to his senses. His hatred temporarily subsided, but within days the evil spirit returned. Saul, having rejected the Holy Spirit's rule in his heart, had no protection from the voice of darkness ringing in his ears. It whispered. It planted suspicions. It maliciously fueled the fires of envy. It tormented the man with constant fear.

A few days later, as David tried to soothe away the king's vexing fears with the calming music of his harp, Saul snapped again and hurled his spear at the young man. Now that the handwriting on the wall was unmistakably clear to David, he would have to flee for his life. Before departing, he arranged a clandestine encounter with his friend Jonathan. The two wept as they separated, "but David wept more." (I Samuel 20:41) Not only did it mean he had to run for his life, but it also meant abandoning everything that was dear to him: his wife, his home, his best friend, his family, his position, his men, and maybe most keenly missed of all, the altars of God. In short, the young man was being stripped of everything. Only that morning, he had been the darling of Israel, hero of the land, son-in-law of the king; by evening he was fleeing for his life.

To David, it certainly must have seemed that the Lord had forsaken him. He hadn't, of course, but He was letting the young man feel the reality of his helplessness. It was all part of what God was doing inside David. But in his panicked condition, he began making mistakes. First, he went to the priestly settlement at Nob, where he lied to Ahimelech the priest about his actions. He then ran to Gath—wearing the sword of their dead champion Goliath! Barely escaping there with his life, he penned the immortal words of Psalm 34:

> I will bless the Lord at all times…O magnify the Lord with me, and let us exalt His name together. I sought the Lord, and He answered me, and delivered me from all my fears. …This poor man cried, and the Lord heard him and saved him out of all his troubles. The angel of the Lord encamps around those who fear Him, and rescues them. O taste and see that the Lord is good; how blessed is the man who takes refuge in Him! …The righteous cry, and the Lord hears and delivers them out of all their troubles. The Lord is near to the brokenhearted and saves those who are crushed in spirit. Many are the afflictions of the righteous, but the Lord delivers him out of them all.

WEEK 7: GOD'S WISDOM

Monday

1. Read and meditate on Psalm 119:89-96 (supplemental reading: Psalm 62).

2. Write out Psalm 119:89.

3. Write out Matthew 24:35.

4. What similarities do you see in these two verses?

5. Scripture utilizes the same term for the eternal realm of Jehovah and the starry universe. Explain any difference you see between the way David and Jesus used the word *heaven*.

6. Read the following comments on Psalm 119:89 and explain what you learn from each of them.

    "After tossing about on a sea of trouble the Psalmist here leaps to shore and stands upon a rock. Jehovah's word is not fickle nor uncertain; it is settled, determined, fixed, sure, immovable. Man's teachings change so often that there is never time for them to be settled; but the Lord's word is from of old the same, and will remain unchanged eternally... In the former section David's soul fainted, but here the good man looks out of self and perceives that the Lord fainteth not, neither is weary, neither is there any failure in his word."[1]

Monday - continued

"Thy purposes are all settled above, and they shall all be fulfilled below."[2]

"The heavens of creation declare the eternal order of the spiritual heavens."[3]

"Whenever you look to heaven, remember that within you there is a God, who has fixed his residence and shown his glory there, and made it the seat both of his mercy and justice. You have also there a Savior who, after he had died for our sins, sat down at the right hand of Majesty, to see his promises accomplished, and by his word to subdue the whole world. There are angels that 'do his commandment, hearkening to the voice of his word' (Psalm 103:20). There are glorified saints, who see God face to face, and dwell with him for evermore, and came there by the same covenant which is propounded to us. In the outer region of heaven we see the sun and moon, and all the heavenly bodies, move in that fixed course and order wherein God hath set them; and will God show his constancy in the course of nature, and be fickle and changeable in the covenant of grace, wherein he has disposed the order and method of his mercies?"[4]

Tuesday

1. Read and meditate on Psalm 119:89-96 (supplemental reading: Psalm 19).

2. Rewrite Psalm 119:90-91 in your own words.

3. How do you see these verses speaking of the sovereignty and faithfulness of God?

4. Please read the following story:

> In 1978, the Israeli intelligence agency, Mossad, discovered that France had agreed to help Iraq build a nuclear reactor. Perceiving the danger of Iraqi strongman Saddam Hussein gaining nuclear capability, they immediately launched Operation Sphinx. Eight separate teams of intelligence specialists were sent to Paris where the work was being done. A preliminary investigation identified an Iraqi scientist named Halim as their best target.
>
> Field supervisors arrived from Tel Aviv to oversee the massive operation of 50 special agents. Safe houses were secured, surveillance crews stalked Halim and his wife, electronic specialists bugged their house and phones, and finally, when everything else was in place, the primary contact team arrived to begin their phase of the operation. These were the people who would have direct contact with the two Iraqis.
>
> Over the course of the next several months, intelligence officers ingratiated themselves with the unsuspecting scientist. They manipulated, they cajoled, they provided prostitutes, they gave him money, all the while dangling the possibility of untold riches before him. In the end, he gave them all the information they were after.
>
> Using this information, the Israeli air force was able to pinpoint their bombs on the reactor located within the Iraqi power plant, thereby destroying Saddam Hussein's ability to produce nuclear weapons.
>
> This interesting spy story provides a wonderful illustration of how intimately and intricately God is involved in the lives of His people. He has made a tremendous investment in every believer's life and is greatly interested in every aspect of it. He loves His children and it is the joy of His great heart to be involved with the details of their lives. The massive Mossad operation, in all its complexity, demonstrates how a person can be the subject of the most intense interest by a host of people without any comprehension of what is going on around him. This story demonstrates the Lord's great involvement in the lives of His people, while they remain largely oblivious to it.[5]

Tuesday - continued

5. Please write out the following verses.
   a. Psalm 33:18

   b. Psalm 139:17-18

   c. Matthew 10:30

6. In Psalm 119:95 one can see the mortal danger in which David lived. Ruthless men were trying to kill him. Explain why you think he felt secure.

Wednesday

1. Read and meditate on Psalm 119:97-104 (supplemental reading: Psalm 25).

2. Write out the phrases from the following verses:

    a. Psalm 119:98a

    b. Psalm 119:99a

    c. Psalm 119:100a

3. "Disciples of Christ who sit at his feet are often better skilled in divine things than doctors of divinity," C.H. Spurgeon rightly said. This is a spiritual truth that the learned often miss. Look up John 7:15-17 and explain the spiritual principle given.

4. Psalm 25:14 offers another true Scriptural principle. The Living Bible really brings out the full meaning: "Friendship with God is reserved for those who reverence him. With them alone he shares the secrets of his promises." Look up the following verses and explain what you learn from each.

    Deuteronomy 29:29

Wednesday - continued

Psalm 111:10

Proverbs 1:23

Proverbs 3:32b

Proverbs 28:5

Jeremiah 33:3

Daniel 2:21b-22

Amos 3:7

Matthew 13:11

Thursday

1. Read and meditate on Psalm 119:97-104 (supplemental reading: Psalm 52).

2. Write out the phrases of the following verses:

    a. Psalm 119:97b

    b. Psalm 119:98b

    c. Psalm 119:99b

    d. Psalm 119:100b

    e. Psalm 119:101a

    f. Psalm 119:102a

3. Psalm 119:98a, 99a and 100a describe the marvelous benefits of spending time in and obeying the word of God. Please review the Scripture phrases you just wrote out and explain how each one contributed to David's godly wisdom.

    a. Psalm 119:97b

    b. Psalm 119:98b

    c. Psalm 119:99b

    d. Psalm 119:100b

    e. Psalm 119:101a

    f. Psalm 119:102a

Friday

1. Read and meditate on Psalm 119:97-104 (supplemental reading: Psalm 57).

2. Write out Psalm 119:103.

3. How do you think David got to the point where Scripture became so enjoyable to him? Do you think it would be equally so had he lived in modern America and continually immersed himself in the Internet and television? Explain your answer.

4. Write out Psalm 119:104.

5. Can you see how continually filling your mind with the unadulterated truth of Scripture would create in you a hatred for falsehood? Explain your answer.

6. Read Psalm 119:97-100 in the supplied versions and describe any new insights that come to you through each translation.

    a. "O how I love your law! All day long I meditate on it. Your commandments make me wiser than my enemies, for I am always aware of them. I have more insight than all my teachers, for I meditate on your rules. I am more discerning than those older than I, for I observe your precepts." (NET)

    b. "Oh, how love I Your law! It is my meditation all the day. You, through Your commandments, make me wiser than my enemies, for [Your words] are ever before me. I have better understanding and deeper insight than all my teachers, because Your testimonies are my meditation. I understand more than the aged, because I keep Your precepts [hearing, receiving, loving, and obeying them]." (AMP)

Saturday

1. Read and meditate on Psalm 119:89-104 (supplemental reading: Psalm 142).

2. Review the story provided in Tuesday's homework. The fact of the matter is that God has been deeply involved with your life since your birth. You have been the focus of an immense heavenly operation for many years. Who can know the number of angels assigned at various times to watch over you? Who can guess how many people God has used in a myriad of ways to influence and mold your life, to bring you to the point of seeing your great need for Him? How many different circumstances of your life—loss, failures, problems, difficult people—did God use to bring you to that momentous decision? In light of this, please read Matthew 6:25-34 and explain why you can trust the Lord to take care of every aspect of your life.

3. Dear one, are you content to know God from afar or are you determined to know Him intimately? Are you satisfied with "the fringes of His ways," or are you one who is hungry to really see the marvels of His kingdom? Look again at the phrases in Thursday's homework. These are the sorts of activities that bring a person into the kind of intimate knowledge God reserves for the hungry. Ponder each of these and honestly describe how much you actually do this in your daily life. What changes should you make in your life so that these verses would be true for you as well?

    a. Psalm 119:97b

    b. Psalm 119:98b

    c. Psalm 119:99b

    d. Psalm 119:100b

    e. Psalm 119:101a

    f. Psalm 119:102a

DAVID IN THE WILDERNESS
I Samuel 22

David, having fled for his life from Saul and then from the Philistines in Gath, finds shelter about 10 miles away in a cave located outside the town of Adullum (Ironically, this cave overlooked the scene of David's greatest triumph, the Valley of Elah). As he sat in this dark, dank hole in the side of a hill, having lost everything dear to him, he got out his pen and wrote Psalm 142, which provides deeper insight into the faith of this young man.

There is no one who regards me; there is no escape for me; no one cares for my soul. I cried out to You, O Lord; I said, "You are my refuge, my portion in the land of the living. Give heed to my cry, for I am brought very low; deliver me from my persecutors, for they are too strong for me. Bring my soul out of prison, so that I may give thanks to Your name; the righteous will surround me, for You will deal bountifully with me." (Psalm 142)

David was all alone, and yet, in faith and desperation he cried out for God to bring "the righteous" to him. And this is exactly what happened. As soon as they heard of his whereabouts, his family slipped away from Bethlehem and joined him in Adullum. Soon, more people arrived. Saul's reign had become exactly what Samuel had predicted of it, best summed up in the first words of I Samuel 8:14: "He will take the best…" And so he did. The selfish monarch grabbed the best from his people for himself and his henchmen. Many of the 400 societal rejects and misfits that made up David's army had been victims of Saul's tyranny.

The small, newly-formed militia, sensing their extreme vulnerability at Adullum, immediately set out for Moab, whose king gave them a warm welcome. Of course, Jesse's grandmother had been Ruth the Moabitess, so he was with his kinfolk there. It seemed like the perfect solution to David's dilemma: he could stay in Moab with his family and be secure from all of his enemies. But it was not God's will for David to remain in this idyllic situation.

Before long, a young "seer" named Gad arrived.

He and David had probably been acquainted in Samuel's school of the prophets years before; indeed, it was probably the old prophet himself who sent him. In any case, Gad informed David that the Lord did not want him to remain in Moab so he obediently left his family in the care of the king while he and his men crossed the Jordan back into the wilds of Judea. It is clear that the Lord purposed a life as a fugitive for David, thus forcing him to learn to depend upon Him for everything: something that would never happen in the security of Moab.

Just a few miles north, Saul sat in his primitive fortress surrounded by Benjaminites he considered trustworthy. As is usual with paranoid dictators, the ones tapped for leadership in their unstable regimes aren't those most qualified for the job, nor those who would best represent the different parts of the country, but those who would remain loyal to the despot no matter what. As in the recent case of Saddam Hussein and other despots like him, family members understand that if the ruler is overthrown, they will lose everything as well.

Throughout the Psalms, one observes David repeatedly speaking of his "enemies." It is interesting to note, however, that he never considered Saul to be his enemy. He was his loyal subject to the very end. But the king had surrounded himself with self-serving men who played on Saul's debilitating fears. They perpetuated his paranoia for their own selfish interests. David aptly described them as "men of wicked lips."

This explains why, when David had the opportunity to kill Saul in the cave of En Gedi, he refused to do it. In fact, his men were apparently so weary of running for their lives and living in caves that they were going to kill the king themselves, despite David's reticence. But David convinced them to spare Saul's life. And so we see into the heart of this young man—a man after God's own heart—who served as protector for his enemy. He truly was a type of Christ.

WEEK 8 : STAYING TRUE

Monday

1. Read and meditate on Psalm 119:105-112 (supplemental reading: Psalm 36).

2. Write out Psalm 119:105.

3. Write out Psalm 119:130.

4. From David's vantage point, he saw a world immersed in spiritual darkness. With the pathway before him obscured, he sensed his acute need for an external source of illumination. He looked to Scripture to help him stay true to the narrow way. Look up the following verses and explain what you learn about light and darkness from each.

    Psalm 36:9

    Psalm 43:3

    Proverbs 4:18

Monday - *continued*

Matthew 22:13

Luke 22:53

John 8:12

Romans 1:21

Ephesians 4:17-18

Ephesians 6:12

I John 1:5-7

Tuesday

1. Read and meditate on Psalm 119:105-112 (supplemental reading: Psalm 78).

2. Write out Psalm 119:111-112.

3. David and the other psalmists use the word *heart* 127 times in the Psalms. What does that tell you about this book of the Bible?

4. Look up the following verses from Psalms and describe what the person's heart does. Please be sure to use your own words. Watch for *contrasting characteristics*.

   Psalms 17:10

   Psalms 28:7

   Psalms 36:1

   Psalms 41:6

   Psalms 45:1

   Psalms 53:1

   Psalms 73:7

   Psalms 77:6

   Psalms 78:8

   Psalms 78:18

   Psalms 78:37

   Psalms 84:2

Wednesday

1. Read and meditate on Psalm 119:105-112 (supplemental reading: Psalm 107).

2. Write out Psalm 119:110.

3. Look up the word *astray* (Heb. *tâ'âh*₈₅₈₂) in a Bible dictionary and list some of the synonyms provided.

4. Look up the following verses that use this Hebrew word and explain what you learn.

   II Chronicles 33:9

   Psalm 95:10

   Psalm 107:4

   Psalm 107:40

   Proverbs 7:25

   Proverbs 10:17

   Proverbs 12:26

   Proverbs 21:16

   Isaiah 53:6

   Jeremiah 23:13

Thursday

1. Read and meditate on Psalm 119:113-120 (supplemental reading: Psalm 65).

2. Write out Psalm 119:118.

3. Write out Psalm 119:21.

4. Explain what you learn from the previous two verses.

5. Look up the word *wander* (Heb. *shâgâh*$_{7686}$) in a Bible dictionary and list some of the synonyms provided.

6. Look up the following verses that use this Hebrew word and explain what you learn.
   Deuteronomy 27:18

   I Samuel 26:21

   Job 6:24

   Proverbs 5:22-23

   Proverbs 19:27

   Proverbs 28:10

7. Write out Psalm 119:10 in your own words as a personal prayer.

Friday

1. Read and meditate on Psalm 119:113-120 (supplemental reading: Psalm 91).

2. Write out Psalm 119:114.

3. Interestingly, this verse sits precisely halfway between the verses which mention those who go astray or wander away (110 & 118). Can you see any correlation between a person making God his hiding place and remaining faithful? Explain your answer.

4. Look up the term *hiding place* (Heb. *sithrâh*5643) in a Bible dictionary and list some of the synonyms provided which would be applicable to the Lord.

5. Look up the following verses that use this Hebrew word and explain what you learn.

    Psalm 27:5

    Psalm 31:20

Friday - continued

Psalm 32:7

Psalm 61:4

Psalm 91:1

6. Compare the different Bible translations provided below for Psalm 119:118. What fresh insights are revealed to you in each of these translations?

   a. "You regard with contempt all who deviate from Your commandments, for their cunning is of no avail." (HAR)

   b. "All who swerve from thy will, thou spurnest; their notions end in nothing." (MOF)

   c. "But you have rejected all who stray from your principles. They are only fooling themselves." (NLT)

Saturday

1. Read and meditate on Psalm 119:105-120 (supplemental reading: Psalm 54).

2. David mentions the heart 15 times in Psalm 119. In your own words, rewrite the phrase containing the word heart in each of these verses as an expression from you to the Lord. Avoid using the word heart if at all possible.

    Psalm 119:2 e.g.: *How spiritually fulfilled are those who pursue God with everything in them.*

    Psalm 119:7

    Psalm 119:10

    Psalm 119:11

    Psalm 119:32

    Psalm 119:34

    Psalm 119:36

    Psalm 119:58

Saturday - continued

Psalm 119:69

Psalm 119:70

Psalm 119:80

Psalm 119:111

Psalm 119:112

Psalm 119:145

Psalm 119:161

3. Look up Isaiah 29:13. Explain its meaning in your own words.

Sunday

MISTAKES
I Samuel 23-30

David spent the next several years living with his men, west of the Dead Sea in the Judean wilderness. One day he received the disheartening message that Samuel had died, news which apparently caused him to begin drifting away from the Lord, and making poor and even ungodly decisions.

The first of these revolved around a disagreement with a rich sheepherder named Nabal, whom David had protected from marauding bands of Amalekites. When it came time for the shepherds to shear their sheep and sell their wool, David sent some of his men to Nabal, seeking the compensation customary in such situations. The gnarly old rancher insulted them instead and sent them away empty-handed.

Incensed, David set out with 400 of his men, determined to kill every male in Nabal's camp. Meanwhile, Nabal's wise and beautiful wife Abigail gathered provisions and rushed them to David. David, both placated and smitten, turned back. A few days later, Nabal suddenly, and inexplicably, died and David asked Abigail to become his wife. Not only did he give himself over to extreme vengeance, but he took a second wife, something which was surely displeasing to the Lord.

But his next mistake was far more serious. One day, we are told, he said to *himself*, "Now I will perish one day by the hand of Saul. There is nothing better for me than to escape into the land of the Philistines." (I Samuel 27:1) In times past, whenever David faced an important decision, he always "inquired of the Lord." Now we find him making impetuous decisions without seeking any guidance from the Lord. His words, "There is nothing better for me…" seems to show that he was growing weary of the difficult path God had laid out for him. He would now, in obvious unbelief, take matters into his own hands.

David and his (now) 600 men went to Achish, king of Gath. The last time David had been there, he barely escaped with his life. Now he and his army were welcomed as celebrated allies and given the town of Ziklag in which to live. Thus began a period of 16 months where the small army enjoyed the comfort and security of city life, as opposed to the hardships of the wilderness. It is an interesting side note that the evidence suggests David wrote no Psalms during this period of his life. It seems that the well had dried up.

Nevertheless, the men settled into their new life of comfort. The provision of sustenance for 600 men and their families compelled David and his men to raid Amalekite, Geshurite and Girzite settlements in the Negev. However, he told Achish that he was attacking Jewish towns so that he would think that David was now their enemy. To ensure that his actual actions were kept secret, he killed every single inhabitant of the towns he raided. It would be one thing if God had told him to do this as an act of judgment, but it seems he committed wholesale slaughter of people simply to protect his own interests.

David drifted further from God's will every day he spent with the Philistines. His deception finally overtook him when Achish announced that they would all be going north to attack the Israelite army. David acted as though he would fight alongside the Philistines, but he knew he was in deep trouble. At this point, God stepped in and bailed him out by causing the other Philistine lords to order him to return to Ziklag.

David and his men made the long march south back to their camp. Upon arriving, they discovered to their horror that a group of Amalekites had raided Ziklag and carried off their wives and children into slavery. His men were so upset with him that they actually contemplated stoning him.

David's protracted period of backsliding and self-will had almost ended in disaster. However, God used this dilemma to bring him to his knees. After a long absence from His presence, we are told that David "strengthened himself in the Lord his God." (I Samuel 30:6) Now, instead of concocting his own plans, David once again "inquired of the Lord." The men attacked the Amalekites and retrieved their families. More importantly, their commander had found his way back into the will of God.

WEEK 9: REDEEM ME FROM MY OPPRESSOR

Monday

1. Read and meditate on Psalm 119:121-128 (supplemental reading: Psalm 7).

2. Write out Psalm 119:126.

3. Scattered throughout the Psalms are what have been coined Imprecatory Psalms. The following list includes most, if not all, of them: Psalm 7, 35, 55, 59, 69, 79, 109, 137 and 139. These Psalms, most of which are Davidic, either in whole or part contain expressions of righteous indignation over the abounding wickedness around him, even calling upon God to destroy His enemies. The strong language employed seems to contradict the New Testament teachings that believers should love their enemies. However, to properly comprehend what was expressed, the Bible student must take certain things into consideration. Ponder the following factors and write out how they affect your understanding of this subject.

   • A longing for the vindication of God's righteousness
   • A zeal for God's kingdom
   • An expression of the Lord's hatred of sin

   • A call for God's judgment of the wicked
   • A call to the wicked to repent
   • A call to the righteous to praise God for His justice

4. Now, in light of what you have just learned, take a look at the following verses where David talks about the wicked and explain what you learn.

   Psalm 119:21

   Psalm 119:53

   Psalm 119:113

   Psalm 119:115

   Psalm 119:118

   Psalm 119:119

   Psalm 119:155

   Psalm 119:158

Tuesday

1. Read and meditate on Psalm 119:121-128 (supplemental reading: Psalm 79).

2. Write out Psalm 119:121b.

3. Write out Psalm 119:134a.

4. David not only refers to wicked people in general in his writings, but also regularly speaks of those who oppressed him personally. According to the two verses above, how did David handle his sufferings at the hands of others?

5. Read the following verses and briefly describe David's response to the situation.

   Psalm 119:51

   Psalm 119:61

   Psalm 119:69

   Psalm 119:70

   Psalm 119:86

   Psalm 119:87

   Psalm 119:95

   Psalm 119:110

   Psalm 119:157

   Psalm 119:161

6. Some people get angry with the Lord when they are treated poorly by others. How would you characterize David's attitude toward the Lord in the face of persecution?

Wednesday

1. Read and meditate on Psalm 119:121-128 (supplemental reading: Psalm 109).

2. Write out Psalm 119:124.

3. Write out Psalm 119:132.

4. Write out Psalm 119:135.

5. In light of these verses and the danger in which he lived, would you say that David trusted himself or God to watch over his life?

6. Read the following account from the life of David in I Samuel 24:1-7 and, in light of what you have learned this week, explain how he handled his enemy.

7. Read the following passages and explain what you learn about dealing with one's enemies from a New Testament perspective.

    Luke 6:27-38

    Romans 12:17-21

    I Peter 2:21-23

Thursday

1. Read and meditate on Psalm 119:129-136 (supplemental reading: Psalm 137).

2. Write out Psalm 119:136.

3. Write out Psalm 119:53.

4. Write out Psalm 119:113.

5. Only a person who is truly separated from this evil world system can comprehend the powerful emotions expressed by David in these verses. A proper understanding of his hatred and "burning indignation" is only possible for those who have experienced what it means to weep over the wickedness around them. Anger or indignation over others' sin, if not coupled with much earnest intercession for them, is nothing more than an expression of self-righteousness. We get a glimpse of "righteous indignation" in the life of Jesus. Read Luke 19:41-46 and explain what you learn about Jesus' emotions.

6. This same godly sorrow toward wickedness is seen in the lives of others as well. Read Jeremiah 9:2-5 and explain what he saw taking place around him.

Thursday - continued

7. Now write out Jeremiah 9:1.

8. Look up Philippians 3:18-19 and explain what you learn about Paul.

9. A life of intercession is unquestionably a life of suffering. This partially explains why Jesus was called a "man of sorrows." And yet, while the God-filled person certainly experiences grief over sin, at the same time he also experiences a deep sense of inner joy. These conflicting passions are not indicative of a person who is emotionally out-of-control. Rather, they are the undeniable manifestation of the strong presence of the Holy Spirit. Yes, Jesus experienced intense grief over the hardness of heart of those around Him. Tempered with that, however, was such joy and peace that children felt free to run into His loving arms. Read Psalm 126:5 and explain what you learn.

Friday

1. Read and meditate on Psalm 119:129-136 (supplemental reading: Psalm 30).

2. Write out Psalm 119:129.

3. Please read the following commentary and then explain David's statement in verse 129.

> The whole word of God, the Scriptures of truth, are his testimonies: they testify of the mind of God, and of his love and grace in the method of salvation by Christ; they testify of Christ, his person, offices, and grace; of the sufferings of Christ, and the glory that should follow; and of all the happiness that comes to the people of God thereby. The law is called a testimony, which being put into the ark, that had the name of the ark of the testimony. This is a testimony of the perfections of God, his holiness, justice, and goodness displayed in it; and of his good and perfect will, what should or should not be done. The Gospel is the testimony of Christ, of what he is, has done and suffered for his people, and of the blessings of grace by him...[1]

4. Write out Psalm 119:130.

5. Please read the following commentary and then explain David's statement in verse 130.

> No sooner do they gain admission into the soul than they enlighten it, what light may be expected from their prolonged indwelling! Their very entrance floods the mind with instruction, for they are so full, so clear; but, on the other hand, there must be such an "entrance," or there will be no illumination. The mere hearing of the word with the external ear is of small value by itself, but when the words of God enter into the chambers of the heart then light is scattered on all sides. The word finds no entrance into some minds because they are blocked up with self-conceit, or prejudice, or indifference; but where due attention is given, divine illumination must surely follow upon knowledge of the mind of God. Oh, that thy words, like the beams of the sun, may enter through the window of my understanding, and dispel the darkness of my mind![2]

Friday - continued

6. Compare the two Bible translations provided below for Psalm 119:129-130. What fresh concepts are revealed to you in each of these translations?

   a. "Thy instruction is wonderful; therefore I gladly keep it. Thy word is revealed, and all is light; it gives understanding even to the untaught." (NEB)

   b. "Your testimonies are wonderful [far exceeding anything conceived by man]; therefore my [penitent] self keeps them [hearing, receiving, loving, and obeying them]. The entrance and unfolding of Your words give light; their unfolding gives understanding (discernment and comprehension) to the simple." (AMP)

Saturday

1. Read and meditate on Psalm 119:121-136 (supplemental reading: Psalm 35).

2. Throughout the Psalms, David mentions his enemies. New Testament saints have been given, through the gift of the Holy Spirit, a fuller revelation about the spiritual warfare that goes on around us. Look up the following verses and briefly explain what you learn.

    II Corinthians 10:3-4

    Ephesians 6:12

3. Many of David's prayers about his enemies can be employed by the Christian in regards to demonic enemies. Read Psalm 35:4-6, 15-28 and rewrite his prayer fitting it into your own situation.

4. Look up the following two passages and briefly explain what you learn.

    Isaiah 59:16

    Ezekiel 22:30

5. A distinct difference exists between intercession and simply praying for another person. While the latter is done out of a sense of concern for the person, the former is a powerful experience brought on by the Holy Spirit. A believer who enters into intercession, in some inexplicable way, spiritually steps into the other person's situation and undertakes his need before God. Have you ever really interceded for another person? I would like to challenge you to make a commitment to the Lord to do the following every morning for the next month.

    a. Ask God to give you an intercessor's heart.

    b. Choose someone you have a burden for and spend five minutes a day bringing their need before the throne of God.

DAVID BECOMES THE KING
I Samuel 28—II Samuel 5

As David and his men headed toward the shock awaiting them in Ziklag, Saul learned, to his utter dismay, that the Philistines were amassing their forces in the Jezreel Valley. He prayed, he went to prophets and visited priests, desperately trying to inquire of the Lord—but the heavens were silent.

Matthew Henry rightly asks: "Could he that hated and persecuted Samuel and David, who were both prophets, expect to be answered by prophets? Could he that had slain the high priest, expect to be answered by Urim? Or could he that had sinned away the Spirit of grace, expect to be answered by dreams?"[3]

Finally, in an act of desperation revealing all too clearly his deranged mental state, Saul visited a medium. The woman agreed to conjure up the spirit of Samuel—but this was no impersonating demon, rather the prophet himself. His words sent a chill through the rebel king. "Why then do you ask me, since the Lord has departed from you and has become your adversary? The Lord has torn the kingdom out of your hand and given it to David… Tomorrow you and your sons will be with me!" (I Samuel 28:16-19)

The very next day the Philistines did indeed ravage the forces of Israel. After a 40-year reign marked by self-will and rebellion, Saul finally went to face his judgment. Tragically, Jonathan, loyal prince and son to the end, was killed alongside him.

David heard the news only two days after returning from his pursuit and subsequent victory over the Amalekites. The Psalmist sang a dirge of sorrow for his fallen king and his beloved friend. After a period of mourning, we once again see those blessed words, indicating the renewed health of his spiritual condition: "Then it came about afterwards that David inquired of the Lord…" (II Samuel 2:1)

And the Lord told him to go to Hebron. In 1011 B.C., at 30 years of age, David of Bethlehem was anointed king of the southern tribe of Judah. However, much unrest and turmoil remained from Saul's tattered regime. Abner, Saul's general, had regrouped his troops in Gilead. Unwilling to relinquish his power and recognize David as king of Israel, he installed as king Ishbosheth, a weak-willed son of Saul.

A long and costly war ensued between David's men and the northern army of Abner. "David grew steadily stronger, but the house of Saul grew weaker continually." (II Samuel 3:1) Eventually, Abner had a disagreement with Ishbosheth and arranged to bring David in as king of the entire nation.

With all of Israel now under his command, David had an important decision to make—where to set up his government. Remaining in Hebron only to repeat the same mistakes Saul made, isolating himself from the other tribes deep within the territory of his own tribe, was not an option. Yet, he also didn't want to foolishly leave his established base of power. Then he set his sights on Jerusalem, a little-known stronghold of a small heathen tribe called the Jebusites, conveniently situated right on the border between the territories of Judah and Benjamin.

David was also attracted to some other notable features of this seemingly insignificant city. Astride the adjoining hills of Moriah and Zion, Jerusalem was surrounded by three steep ravines. It also possessed an unlimited supply of water resulting from an underground spring within its walls. Consequently, it was one of the most easily defensible cities in all of Palestine.

Jerusalem also had promising economic potential because of its proximity: it sat right on the crossroads of two ancient trade routes. One of the main caravan routes of the Middle East ran from the coastal area, up to Jerusalem, down to Jericho, across the Jordan River, over to Amman and on to points east. The other road came from Beersheba and Hebron in the south, along the mountain ridges, past Jerusalem, Bethel and Shiloh, and then up into Galilee.

There was one more important consideration in taking Jerusalem: its inhabitants were heathens, having been allowed to remain because of Saul's poor national leadership. Had it been a Jewish city, a large part of its residents would have been displaced by the hundreds of soldiers and their families who needed to live near the king.

Sunday - continued

And, of course, it goes without saying that Zion was the chosen city of God.

> For the Lord has chosen Zion; He has desired it for His habitation. "This is My resting place forever; here I will dwell, for I have desired it." (Psalm 132:13-14)

> Great is the Lord, and greatly to be praised, in the city of our God, His holy mountain. Beautiful in elevation, the joy of the whole earth, is Mount Zion in the far north, the city of the great King. (Psalm 48:1-2)

> "May they prosper who love you." (Psalm 122:6)

WEEK 10: SMALL AND DESPISED

Monday

1. Read and meditate on Psalm 119:137-144 (supplemental reading: Psalm 11).

2. Write out Psalm 119:137.

3. David, like all those with a real sight of God, understood that the Lord's righteousness was infinitely greater than his own. People must typically go through much humbling to have any real grasp of God's righteousness because, frankly, we humans tend to think so highly of ourselves. We cannot see beyond our own level of goodness, thus everyone else is measured by the shortsighted standards established by our own lives. Quickly breeze over the story found in Luke 18:9-14 and describe what you learn about a person's opinion of his own righteousness (apart from God).

4. There is such a thing as a righteous life, but it is not found in SELF; it only comes forth as the Holy Spirit lives God's righteousness in and through us. Look up the following phrases and briefly describe how that happens.

    Psalm 37:30a

    Proverbs 10:11a

    Proverbs 10:20a

    Proverbs 10:21a

Monday - *continued*

Proverbs 10:31a

Proverbs 10:32a

Proverbs 11:30a

Proverbs 28:1b

5. Look up the following verses and describe the blessing that comes from a righteous life.

Psalm 5:12

Psalm 11:7

Psalm 34:15

Proverbs 15:9b

Matthew 5:6

James 5:16

1. Read and meditate on Psalm 119:137-144 (supplemental reading: Psalm 8).

2. Write out Psalm 119:141.

3. Look up I Samuel 15:17 and describe what you learn from the life of Saul.

4. Saul had been "small in [his] own sight" at one time, but gradually became very huge in his own mind. When a person thinks this way, he is quick to take credit for the good that happens in his life because God has become small in his mind. Thus, he elevates himself and refuses to glorify God. (Romans 1:21) On the other hand, the person who is little in his own sight sees God in everything and is quick to give Him glory. Do you agree with these statements? Explain your answer.

5. Please read the following passage and explain what you learn about pride.

   Unquestionably, pride is one of the most prominent subjects addressed in Scripture. The Bible uses at least 17 different words (and countless derivatives) to describe this spiritual disease. However, no matter which term is used, there is almost always a connotation of height: something high, rising, exalted, or being lifted up. Thus, a proud person has a high estimation of himself and lifts himself above those around him. This concept of self-exaltation forms the basis for our working definition of pride: *Having an exaggerated sense of one's own importance and a selfish preoccupation with one's own rights.* It is the attitude that says, "I am more important than you and, if need be, I will promote my cause and protect my rights at your expense."[1]

Tuesday - continued

6. Look up the following verses and describe what happens to the proud person.

   a. Proverbs 11:2a

   b. Proverbs 16:18a

   c. Proverbs 16:18b

   d. Matthew 23:12a

7. Peter was a man who underwent a great deal of God's chastisement. He understood the tremendous value of allowing the Lord to humble him. Look up I Peter 5:5-6 and list 6 things you learn about pride and humility.

   a.

   b.

   c.

   d.

   e.

   f.

Wednesday

1. Read and meditate on Psalm 119:145-152 (supplemental reading: Psalm 72).

2. Write out the following phrases.

    Psalm 119:145a

    Psalm 119:146a

    Psalm 119:147a

    Psalm 119:149

3. The Bible is one long story of a compassionate God who meets the needs of those who humble themselves before Him and cry out for His aid. He is irresistibly drawn to the needy. When we cry out for His help, we are putting ourselves into the enviable position of receiving from God. He has an irrepressible compulsion to help those who ask for help. Look up the following verses and explain what you learn.

    I Samuel 2:8

    Psalm 12:5

    Psalm 69:33

    Psalm 72:12-14

    Psalm 107:6

    Isaiah 25:4

Wednesday - continued

4. Jesus used two stories to teach His disciples to pray. Read each of these anecdotes and describe what you learn.

Luke 11:5-8

Luke 18:1-7

Wednesday - continued

Thursday

1. Read and meditate on Psalm 119:145-152 (supplemental reading: Psalm 39).

2. Write out Psalm 119:145b.

3. This is a declaration of commitment. Something had happened within David's heart to transform him from one who did his own will to one who obeyed God from the heart. By saying the words, "I will," he was expressing his willingness to submit his will to that of God. Read the following passages and explain what you learn about being submitted to God's will.

    Matthew 7:21

    Matthew 12:46-50

    Matthew 21:28-31

    Matthew 26:39

    John 6:38

    Ephesians 6:6

    Hebrews 10:36

    I Peter 4:1-2

    I John 2:17

Thursday - continued

4. Please read the following passage and explain what you learn.

Every human being possesses an innate sense of self-determination and self-sufficiency. When a person becomes a follower of Christ, he has set himself on an unavoidable collision course with the will of God, regardless of the severity of his sin. Indeed, the very entrance into the kingdom of God is founded upon the person seeing that his way has been wrong and must therefore be changed. The biblical term used to describe the solution to this problem is called REPENTANCE.

Many suppose that when they first became Christians they experienced repentance and now they can move on to the more important things of the Christian life. Not only is the initial conversion experience for many very weak, as we shall soon see, but it is only meant to be the first in a lifelong series of such encounters with God. There is much that needs to be changed about the fallen human nature. God is not looking for more people who know how to appear religious or speak the latest "Christianese." He is looking to transform us from the inside out that we may bear the image of Jesus Christ to the unsaved world.

True repentance, then, is much more than aligning oneself with the Christian religion. The Greek word which we translate as repentance is *metanoia*. It is the combination of the words *meta* (after, following) and *noieo* (think). *Metanoia* means to reconsider, or to experience a change in one's line of thinking.

Before we discuss repentance of sexual sin, let us return to the matter of the human will. For a person to think that he can "repent" of any sin, and yet refuse to change his way of thinking is foolish. Spiritual repentance is an experience whereby a person's will is altered for the express purpose of bringing it into line with God's will... .

The only way we can come into meekness is through the breaking of our wills. A perfect picture of this is that of a stallion. It may be a beautiful and graceful animal, but it has no usefulness until it has been broken. However, once it has been broken, the powerful horse becomes controlled by the reins and verbal commands of its master. This is a picture of biblical meekness.

The Christian who has undergone the crushing of his will by his Heavenly Father has learned to have a healthy respect for the Master's whip. This is not the cowering fear an abused child has of a cruel father, but the proper reverence one has to One who commands respect. This man's will has been conquered so that he no longer sees his life as one in which he has the right to control.[2]

Friday

1. Read and meditate on Psalm 119:145-152 (supplemental reading: Psalm 93).

2. Write out Psalm 119:151.

3. Look up the following verses and explain what you learn about drawing near to God.

   Psalm 32:9

   Psalm 34:18

   Psalm 145:18

   Isaiah 29:13

   Hebrews 4:16

   James 4:8a

4. Compare the different Bible translations provided below for Psalm 119:141. What fresh concepts are revealed to you in each of these translations?

   a. "I am unimportant and despised, but I do not neglect your teachings." (GNB)

   b. "I am small and of no account; but I keep your orders in mind." (BBE)

   c. "I am lowly and regarded with contempt, yet I have not forgotten Your precepts." (HAR)

Saturday

1. Read and meditate on Psalm 119:137-152 (supplemental reading: Psalm 60).

2. Where do you see yourself in the story Jesus told in Luke 18:9-14? Would you say that you lean more in the direction of seeing what you are doing right *or* your spiritual lack? Explain yourself.

3. Previously, I defined pride as: *Having an exaggerated sense of one's own importance and a selfish preoccupation with one's own rights.* It is the attitude that says, "I am more important than you and, if need be, I will promote my cause and protect my rights at your expense." Take a good, hard look at the way you go through life, the underlying attitudes you have about other people, the perspectives that dictate your daily decisions, etc. In what ways do you see pride at work in your heart? Are there still areas in your life where you have not allowed God to break your will? What are they? List them.

Saturday - *continued*

4. Please reread the passage of *At the Altar of Sexual Idolatry* found in Thursday's homework. Briefly mention five different occurrences when the Lord did a work of breaking your will.

    a.

    b.

    c.

    d.

    e.

Sunday

DAVID SECURES THE KINGDOM
II Samuel 6—10

David, having captured, secured and built up Jerusalem, initiated an all-encompassing strategy to create national security, establish a legitimate government and lead the Jewish people back into the worship of Jehovah.

As one of his first orders of business, the new king secured Israel's borders. With the recent change in leadership, the nation was very vulnerable to attack. The Israelites had just suffered a terrible defeat by the Philistines and then immediately became embroiled in a civil war. Once David had regained control over the entire kingdom, his first priority was to repay the Philistines for what they had done. Successfully seizing the garrison in Gath, he installed his own troops there to keep them in subjection.

The next nation he dealt with was Moab, whose king had apparently murdered David's parents. This might explain why, after capturing their army, he executed two-thirds of their men. After this he defeated the Edomites to the southeast and the Aramaeans to the north. His last order of business would come later with the Ammonites.

At home in Jerusalem, David set up an administration far superior to the ragtag group of cronies Saul had gathered around himself. He selected gifted leaders over the army, the nation's storehouses, the agriculture and the treasury. He also appointed a private secretary, special advisors and even a personal bodyguard.

Probably the most important area to receive attention was that of religion. In the two hundred years since the death of Joshua, the Jewish people had steadily regressed spiritually. Astonishingly, they had adopted the Canaanite concept of henotheism: the belief that there were many gods and that those gods were more powerful in their own particular geographical areas. Thus, Jehovah was simply the god of the Israelites, just like Molech ruled over the Ammonites. It was very common for Jews to have a shrine to Baal right next to an altar to Jehovah!

David labored tirelessly to bring this double-minded religion to an end. For all his mistakes, personal weaknesses and times of rebellion, he sincerely loved the Lord and almost single-handedly brought His people back to Him.

At the outset of this noble crusade, he first focused his attention on the Ark of the Covenant. The Ark had been sitting neglected in the house of a Levite in Kiriah-Jearim ever since the Philistines had returned it on a cart some 70 years before. David assembled 30,000 Jewish leaders to go there with him and usher it into its rightful place. Unfortunately, in their haste and enthusiasm, they failed to consult Scripture, which provides elaborate instructions on how to move it. Instead, they copied the Philistines and transported it on an oxen cart. As David and the other leaders celebrated in the front of the procession, the cart tipped and one of the men reached out to try to steady it. To everyone's shock, God struck him dead on the spot. It was only later that the man's irreverent attitude came to light. Be that as it may, the merry procession was brought to a halt and everyone returned home. David was sorely disappointed and even angry with the Lord over the incident. What he failed to realize was that, through this incident, God established a fear and sobriety in the nation's leadership which would remain intact for many years to come. Three months later, they brought the Ark by the prescribed method to rest in a newly-built tabernacle in Jerusalem.

Once this was accomplished, David re-established the Levitical priesthood and the sacrificial system. Additionally, he implemented an entire worship department consisting of musicians, psalmists and singers.

Not long after, it entered David's heart to build a magnificent temple for the Lord—something worthy of its Occupant. David's desire to do this pleased the Lord, but this job would, by divine choice, belong to another. Nevertheless, Jehovah made an oath with the king of His people—the Davidic Covenant. It said, in essence, that He would bless David and his people and establish an everlasting throne with his descendents. The ultimate fulfillment of this great promise will be realized through Jesus Christ.

Those first few years of David's reign in Jerusalem would eventually emerge as the highlight of God's 2,000-year relationship with the Jewish people. Thereafter, a disastrous process of deterioration unfolded, beginning with David—in an area of his heart that had never yet been conquered.

WEEK II: REVIVE ME

Monday

1. Read and meditate on Psalm 119:153-160 (supplemental reading: Psalm 71).

2. Write out Psalm 119:154.

3. Look up the word *revive* (Heb. *châyâh*₂₄₂₁) in a Bible dictionary and list some of the synonyms provided.

4. Look up these verses that contain this Hebraic term (*châyâh*): Genesis 5:3, Genesis 17:18 , Deuteronomy 16:20, I Samuel 2:6, II Kings 20:7, Jeremiah 27:17. After you have read all of them, write a one-sentence definition or explanation of it.

5. Every believer experiences periods of spiritual dryness. It's at these times when we need the Lord to breathe fresh life into us. Now look up these verses and explain what you learn.

   Psalm 71:20

   Psalm 80:18

   Psalm 85:6

   Psalm 138:7

   Psalm 143:11

   Isaiah 57:15

   Habakkuk 3:2

Tuesday

1. Read and meditate on Psalm 119:153-160 (supplemental reading: Psalm 42).

2. Write out Psalm 119:156.

3. While the Old Testament uses only one word to describe both physical life and spiritual life, the New Testament makes a differentiation. Read the following passage and explain the difference between the two Greek terms.

    > On another occasion, Jesus slightly altered the second statement: "He who loves his life (Greek, *psyche*) loses it; and he who hates his life (*psyche*) in this world (*kosmos*) shall keep it to life (*zoe*) eternal." (John 12:25) The deliberate choice of words for "life" sheds light on the real meaning. *Psyche* represents one's existence on earth, while *zoe* represents one's life in God. So Jesus was saying that whoever loves **his existence on earth** loses it; and he who hates **his existence in *kosmos*** shall keep it to **a life in God** forevermore."[1]

4. Look up the following NT verses which employ the Greek term *zoe*. Rewrite each one, adding in the adjective phrase, *spiritual and eternal*, before the actual term *life*.

    Matthew 7:14 e.g., For the gate is small and the way is narrow that leads to *spiritual and eternal* life, and there are few who find it.

    John 1:4

    John 10:10

    Colossian 3:3

    II Peter 1:3a

    I John 3:14a

    Revelation 3:5

    Revelation 22:1

Wednesday

1. Read and meditate on Psalm 119:153-160 (supplemental reading: Psalm 86).

2. Write out Psalm 119:159.

3. The Hebrew word *châyâh* is used 16 times in Psalm 119 alone. The literal meaning of this word actually becomes clearer if one uses the term *life* as a verb. In other words, instead of saying, *Revive me...* one would say, *Life me...* Just for the sake of gaining a greater sense of what is being expressed, let's take this exercise one step further. In each of the following verses, replace the words *revive me* with the phrase *life me spiritually and eternally.*

   Psalm 119:25b e.g., *Life me spiritually and eternally* according to Your word.

   Psalm 119:37b

   Psalm 119:40b

   Psalm 119:50b

   Psalm 119:88a

   Psalm 119:93b

   Psalm 119:107b

   Psalm 119:149b

4. In the middle of Paul's prayer for the Ephesian believers, he wrote, "...that He would grant you, according to the riches of His glory, to be strengthened with power through His Spirit in the inner man." (Ephesians 3:16) Can you see any correlation between David's personal appeals mentioned above and Paul's intercession for others?

5. Combine David's and Paul's terminology to write out a prayer to God on your own behalf.

Thursday

1. Read and meditate on Psalm 119:161-168 (supplemental reading: Psalm 64).

2. Write out Psalm 119:164.

3. In this verse David provides a glimpse into his daily life at a particular point in his spiritual journey. What kind of life must he have had in order to maintain this daily discipline? Explain your answer.

4. Write out Psalm 119:165.

5. The Hebrew word for *peace* is *shalom*[7965]; the corresponding Greek term is *eirene*[1515]. Look up the following verses and explain what you learn from each.

   Psalm 29:11

   Proverbs 3:1-2

   Isaiah 9:6

   Isaiah 26:3

   John 14:27

   John 16:33

   Romans 5:1

   Galatians 5:22

   Philippians 4:6-7

Friday

1. Read and meditate on Psalm 119:161-168 (supplemental reading: Psalm 32).

2. Write out Psalm 119:168.

3. Look up the following verses and explain what you learn.

    Psalm 90:8

    Proverbs 5:21

    Proverbs 15:3

    Jeremiah 16:17

    Jeremiah 32:19

    Hebrews 4:13

    Revelation 2:23

Friday - continued

4. Read the following verses taken from *The Living Bible* and write out what you have learned.

   a. Psalm 119:156. "Lord, how great is your mercy; oh, give me back my life again."

   b. Psalm 119:157. "My enemies are so many. They try to make me disobey, but I have no swerved from your will."

   c. Psalm 119:158. "I loathed these traitors because they care nothing for your laws."

   d. Psalm 119:162. "I rejoice in your laws like one who finds a great treasure."

   e. Psalm 119:165. "Those who love your laws have great peace of heart and mind and do not stumble."

Saturday

1. Read and meditate on Psalm 119:153-168 (supplemental reading: Psalm 51).

2. Can you see how there would be times when you need the Lord to breathe fresh life into you spiritually?

3. Have you ever experienced a time when the Lord seemed to draw near to you? How did it affect you?

4. The Christian life is one of balance. There are those who cringe at the thought of a believer having spiritual experiences. Seemingly, they believe that sensing the marvelous presence of God or receiving a powerful revelation were the worst things that could happen to them. They see Christianity as a long road of dry obedience. Look up Psalm 84:1-8 and relate what it expresses to your own experiences.

5. At the opposite end of the spectrum, there are those who attempt to live their lives from one experience to another. Please read the following quotation and explain how what is expressed here has been true in your life.

    The Christian life is not meant to be lived continuously at a fever pitch. Being lost in the exhilaration of God's love or a mountaintop revelation of what He is like can be wonderfully encouraging in a believer's spiritual journey. Nevertheless, Christian growth usually comes from fighting through the thick foliage of life's problems down on the jungle floor, where true godly character is built and where the maturing believer learns what it means to live by faith in God.[2]

Sunday

BATHSHEBA
II Samuel 11-12

The one thing that stands out to me most glaringly about the life of David is how grateful God was to finally have a man on the throne of Israel who loved Him and would lead His people to Him. Seemingly, the Lord couldn't do enough to bless him. How then could the Sweet Psalmist of Israel do something so wicked as what he did with Bathsheba?

As previously mentioned, David's first years on the throne of Israel in Jerusalem were the highpoint of his life and indeed for the entire history of the Jewish nation. With the passage of time, it seems the comfort and security he now enjoyed diminished his sense of need to stay pressed into God. Once again, his inward panting for God's abiding presence slowly began to wane and he lost his intimate connection with the Lord.

Another factor contributing to his loss of spiritual vitality was the pressing weight of responsibility inherent in being king over a nation. However, along with these added duties came a great deal of outward prosperity, to which David now turned for relief *rather than the Lord.*

Further contributing to this backsliding was an insatiable lust for women, lurking and operating unchecked within his breast. By the time he left Hebron, David already had 7 wives, to which he rapaciously added "more concubines and wives from Jerusalem." The truth is that when the affluent king looked down from his balcony and saw Bathsheba, he simply no longer had the inner strength to withstand the temptation to take her for himself.

This one sin, predictably, led to another heinous transgression. A few weeks after the incident, Bathsheba announced that she was pregnant. David attempted to conceal his involvement by bringing Uriah back from the battlefield at Rabbah (modern-day Amman). His hope was that the unwitting husband would have relations with his wife while he was in town, but Uriah refused to sleep with his wife, even after David got him drunk. Foiled in his attempts at duplicity, the hardhearted and desperate king now sent a note back to Joab to put Uriah into the hottest part of the battle where he would surely be killed. After Bathsheba's customary period of mourning, David brought the pregnant woman into his harem to join his other wives.

Months passed and David grew increasingly calloused. He later wrote of that period: "When I kept silent *about my sin,* my body wasted away through my groaning all day long. For day and night Your hand was heavy upon me; my vitality was drained away *as* with the fever heat of summer." (Psalm 32:3-4) Nothing so withers the soul as sin that goes unacknowledged and unrepentant.

David remained in this backslidden condition for a full year while the Lord bided His time. Finally, He sent Nathan (undoubtedly another protégé of Samuel) to the palace under the pretense of seeking judgment on behalf of a poor man who had been ripped off by a rich neighbor. When David heard the story, he ordered the wealthy man to be executed: harsh punishment for a simple theft, and another indication of the king's backslidden condition.

"You are the man!" the prophet woefully exclaimed. "Thus says the Lord God of Israel, 'It is I who anointed you king over Israel and… if that had been too little, I would have added to you many more things like these! Why have you despised the word of the Lord by doing evil in His sight? Now therefore, the sword shall never depart from your house… .'" (II Samuel 12:7-10)

"I have sinned against the Lord," David lamented. "Be gracious to me, O God, according to Your lovingkindness; according to the greatness of Your compassion blot out my transgressions. Wash me thoroughly from my iniquity and cleanse me from my sin. For I know my transgressions, and my sin is ever before me. Against You, You only, I have sinned and done what is evil in Your sight… Do not cast me away from Your presence and do not take Your Holy Spirit from me." (Psalm 51:1-11)

The Lord forgave David his sin. Nonetheless, Bathsheba's child died and the remainder of David's life was marked by hardship, adversity and more failure.

WEEK 12: LET

Monday

1. Read and meditate on Psalm 119:169-176 (supplemental reading: Psalm 68).

2. Write out the following phrases.

    a. Psalm 119:169a

    b. Psalm 119:170a

    c. Psalm 119:171a

    d. Psalm 119:172a

    e. Psalm 119:173a

    f. Psalm 119:175a

    g. Psalm 119:175b

3. Why do you think David used the word "let" ("may" in NIV) so often. What does that tell you about the need for God's help in the transformation of your character? Explain your answers.

Monday - *continued*

4. Write out the following phrases and then answer these questions. Would you say that God was very large in David's consciousness? Would you say that the Lord's sovereignty over his life was real to him?

   Psalm 119:10b

   Psalm 119:116b

   Psalm 119:122b

   Psalm 119:133b

5. What do you think David meant by his statement in Psalm 119:176? Why do you think he ended this great Psalm in such a way?

6. Look at Psalm 119:169-171 in the *New Living Translation* (provided below). What fresh concepts are revealed to you in this passage?

   "O Lord, listen to my cry; give me the discerning mind you promised. Listen to my prayer; rescue me as you promised. Let praise flow from my lips, for you have taught me your decrees." (NLT)

Tuesday

1. Supplemental reading: Psalm 68.

2. Considering all that you have learned over the past eleven weeks, pray-read through the first five stanzas (Psalm 119:1-40). These are inspired prayers. Pray them in faith, believing that God will answer them.

Wednesday

1. Supplemental reading: Psalm 69.

2. Considering all that you have learned over the past eleven weeks, pray-read through the second five stanzas (Psalm 119:41-80). These are inspired prayers. Pray them in faith, believing that God will answer them.

Thursday

1. Supplemental reading: Psalm 70.

2. Considering all that you have learned over the past eleven weeks, pray-read through the third five stanzas (Psalm 119:81-120). These are inspired prayers. Pray them in faith, believing that God will answer them.

Friday

1. Supplemental reading: Psalm 4.

2. Considering all that you have learned over the past eleven weeks, pray-read through the fourth five stanzas (Psalm 119:121-160). These are inspired prayers. Pray them in faith, believing that God will answer them.

Saturday

1. Read and meditate on Psalm 119:161-176 (supplemental reading: Psalm 55).

2. Pick out ten meaningful verses from Psalm 119 and explain why they meant the most to you.

    a.

    b.

    c.

    d.

    e.

    f.

    g.

    h.

    i.

    j.

A REVIEW OF THE LIFE OF DAVID
II Samuel 13-I Kings 2

Sunday

In observing the whole of David's life, two main themes materialize: 1) the blessings that come from intimacy with God, and 2) the consequences of sin.

Perhaps no biblical character exemplified the degree of hunger for God as did David in his early years. Alexander MacLaren wrote of him: "His words have been for ages the chosen expression for the devotions of the holiest souls; and whoever has wished to speak longings after purity, lowly trust in God, the aspirations of love, or the raptures of devotion, has found no words of his own more natural than those of the poet-king of Israel."[1] One need only read the following passages to sense the truth of this statement.

> "One thing I have asked from the Lord, that I shall seek: That I may dwell in the house of the Lord all the days of my life, to behold the beauty of the Lord and to meditate in His temple. For in the day of trouble He will conceal me in His tabernacle; in the secret place of His tent He will hide me; He will lift me up on a rock." (Psalm 27:4-5)

> "O God, You are my God; I shall seek You earnestly; my soul thirsts for You, my flesh yearns for You, in a dry and weary land where there is no water. Thus I have seen You in the sanctuary, to see Your power and Your glory. Because Your lovingkindness is better than life, my lips will praise You." (Psalm 63:1-3)

How gratifying it must have been to the Lord to hear such prayers! And He indeed answered these petitions, first with the ineffable beauty of His presence and secondly, with outward prosperity.

However, juxtaposed against these blessings were the devastating consequences of sin and failure. Seeds of rebellion sown earlier eventually sprouted and corruption blossomed in his latter years. So, even while he enjoyed prosperity, troubles began to surface in "Camelot."

First, Amnon, David's oldest son, born to him through his second wife Ahinoam, raped his half-sister Tamar. Two years later, her brother Absalom murdered him. About seven years later, Absalom attempted to kill his father and wrest the kingdom away from him, eventually being brutally killed himself in battle. The last major recorded event of David's life found him conducting a national census in direct disobedience of the Lord, bringing about a judgment which cost the lives of some 70,000 people.

Not long after, David named Solomon his successor and died at the ripe old age of 70.

For practical application, it is worth mentioning a number of prevailing characteristics of David's life. Let's take a brief look at his weaknesses first:

- Periodic lapses into periods of spiritual complacency and self-trust
- Lust for women
- Occasional times of inordinate harshness

David's strong points as a believer and as a leader far outweigh his weaknesses:

- A sincere love for God
- A deep faith and a great sight of the Lord
- An oft-exhibited magnanimous spirit with others
- A great deal of integrity
- A willingness to accept reproof
- A willingness to repent

In attempting to summarize David's life, I suppose the greatest weight should be placed upon the profound words the Lord used in recalling him to others. To Solomon He said, "If you will walk before Me as your father David walked, in integrity of heart and uprightness…" (I Kings 9:4) About Abijam He said, "His heart was not wholly devoted to the Lord his God, like the heart of his father David." (I Kings 15:3) He told Jeroboam, "My servant David, who kept My commandments and who followed Me with all his heart, to do only that which was right in My sight." (I Kings 14:8) When the dust settled on his life, the truth is that God had nothing but good to say about this shepherd boy turned warrior-king. Yes, David was weak in some ways, had his times of self-satisfaction and even outright rebellion, but the bottom line is that he was a man after God's own heart. I believe that says it all.`

APPENDIX

WEEK 5

Tuesday

5. a.   Joseph's brothers (Genesis 42-45)
         David (II Samuel 12 & Psalm 52; also I Chronicles 21)
         Job (Job 42); Naaman (II Kings 5)
         Manasseh (II Chronicles 33)
         Jonah (Jonah 2)
         Prodigal Son (Luke 15)
         Zaccheus (Luke 19)
         Peter (Matthew 26)

    b.   Pharaoh (Exodus 7-14)
         The Israelites in the wilderness (Psalm 78, I Corinthians 10, Hebrews 3)
         King Saul (I Samuel 15)
         Solomon (I Kings 11)
         Jeroboam (I Kings 14)
         Judas (Matthew 26-27, Acts 1)
         The woman called Jezebel (Revelation 2)

TIMELINE OF PERSONALITIES

Event	Year (BC)	Biblical Reference	Samuel	Saul	David
Samuel born		I Sam. 1	—		
Saul born	1091	n/a	19	—	
Ark taken	1090	I Sam. 5-6	20	1	
Battle at Mizpeh	1070	I Sam. 7	40	21	
Saul becomes king	1053	I Sam. 10	57	38	
Saul's illegal sacrifice	1051	I Sam. 13	59	40	
David born	1041	I Ki. 2:11	69	50	—
Saul & Amalekites	1026	I Sam. 15	84	65	15
David anointed	1026	I Sam. 16	84	65	15
David & Goliath	1021	I Sam. 17	89	70	20
David flees	1019	I Sam. 19	91	72	22
Samuel dies	1015	I Sam. 25	95	76	26
David goes to Gath	1013	I Sam. 27	—	78	28
Saul dies	1011	I Sam. 31		80	30
David king-Hebron	1011	II Sam. 2		—	30
David king-Israel	1004	II Sam. 5			37
David & Bathsheba	991	II Sam. 11			50
Absalom's conspiracy	980	II Sam. 15			61
David dies	971	I Kings 2			70

I Kings 2:11 tells us that David was 30 years old when he became king of the southern tribes, 37 years old when he became king of the entire nation and that he reigned a total of 40 years. Most scholars agree that he became king of Judah in or around 1011 B.C.

Assuming this to be the case, one can estimate dates of key events before, during and after his life. A corruption of I Samuel 13:1 has left Saul's age at ascending the throne in question, but since his son was old enough to lead in battle, it is safe to assume he was at least in his late thirties. Acts 13:21 tells us that he reigned 40 years, but most feel that this was a rounded number and that it was probably 42 years.

The dates provided in this timeline are approximate and should only be used to help the student gain a fuller perspective on the interconnected lives of the relevant individuals.

NOTES

INTRODUCTION

1. D. Martyn Lloyd-Jones, *An Exposition of Ephesians*, Vol. 1 (Grand Rapids, MI: Baker Books, 1978) p. 367.

WEEK 1

1. C.H. Spurgeon, *The Treasury of David* as cited in *AGES Digital Library* (Rio, WI: AGES Software, Inc. 2001).

WEEK 2

1. Steve Gallagher, *At the Altar of Sexual Idolatry* (Dry Ridge, KY: Pure Life Ministries, 2000) pp. 266-267.
2. C.H. Spurgeon.
3. Ibid.

WEEK 3

1. *The Pulpit Commentary: I Samuel* as cited in *AGES Digital Library* (Rio, WI: AGES Software, Inc. 2001).

WEEK 4

1. Steve Gallagher, *Living in Victory* (Dry Ridge, KY: Pure Life Ministries, 2002) p. 84.
2. Steve Gallagher, *Intoxicated with Babylon* (Dry Ridge, KY: Pure Life Ministries, 2005) pp. 183-184.
3. *The Pulpit Commentary: I Samuel*.

WEEK 5

1. Albert Barnes, *Notes on the Bible*, as cited in *AGES Digital Library* (Rio, WI: AGES Software, Inc. 2000).
2. Ibid.
3. *The Pulpit Commentary: I Samuel*.

WEEK 6

1. Steve Gallagher, *At the Altar of Sexual Idolatry*, p. 60.
2. Steve Gallagher, *Living in Victory*, p. 126.

WEEK 7

1. C.H. Spurgeon.
2. Adam Clarke, *Adam Clarke's Commentary on the Bible*, as cited in *AGES Digital Library* (Rio, WI: AGES Software, Inc. 2000).
3. Joseph Morris, *The Biblical Illustrator* as cited in *AGES Digital Library* (Rio, WI: AGES Software, Inc. 2001).
4. Thomas Manton, *The Treasury of David*, as cited in *AGES Digital Library* (Rio, WI: AGES Software, Inc. 2001).
5. Steve Gallagher, adapted from *Living in Victory*, pp. 113-119.

WEEK 9

1. John Gill, *Gill's Exposition of the Entire Bible*, accessed at http://biblehub.com/commentaries/gill/psalms/119-2.htm on May 29, 2014.
2. C.H. Spurgeon, *The Treasury of David* as cited in *AGES Digital Library* (Rio, WI: AGES Software, Inc. 2001).

WEEK 10

1. Steve Gallagher, *Irresistible to God*, (Dry Ridge, KY: Pure Life Ministries, 2003) p. 19.
2. Steve Gallagher, *At the Altar of Sexual Idolatry*, pp. 212-213, 222.

WEEK 11

1. Steve Gallagher, *Intoxicated with Babylon*, p. 193.
2. Steve Gallagher, *Living in Victory*, p. 29.

WEEK 12

1. Alexander MacLaren, *David's Cry for Purity, Whole Bible Sermon Collection* as cited in *AGES Digital Library* (Rio, WI: AGES Software, Inc. 2000).

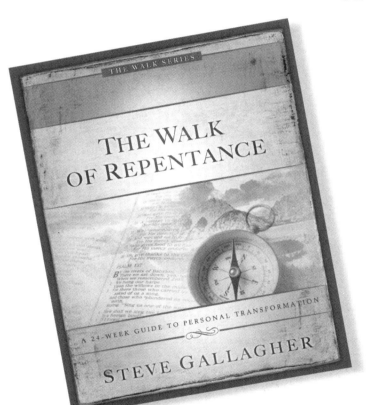

PRESSING ON TOWARD THE HEAVENLY CALLING

A 12-WEEK STUDY THROUGH THE PRISON EPISTLES

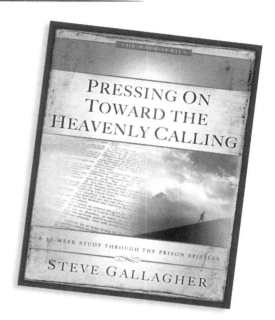

THIS TWELVE-WEEK STUDY OF EPHESIANS, PHILIPPIANS AND COLOSSIANS WILL INSPIRE EVERY BELIEVER TO KEEP "PRESSING ON."

The Prison Epistles are a divine archive of profound revelations about the kingdom of God, accumulated by a man who for many years enjoyed unbroken fellowship with the Lord. For nearly thirty years, the "apostle to the Gentiles" had been pouring out his life and pointing multitudes to Christ. Now, his life and his letters come alive in a practical and personal way. Through this twelve-week study, every believer will be inspired to join Paul's quest in *Pressing On Toward the Heavenly Calling.*

HE LEADS ME BESIDE STILL WATERS

A 12-WEEK STUDY THROUGH THE CHOICEST PSALMS

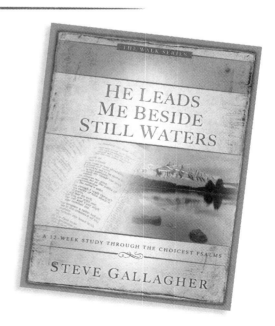

A PRACTICAL STUDY FOR THE HEART THAT SEEKS TO KNOW AND WORSHIP GOD.

"The Book of Praises," as ancient worshipers of Jehovah called the Psalms, is a fitting name for a book in which the adoration of God is the prominent theme. God's glorious attributes are revealed in a variety of ways: His sovereignty, majesty, power, mercy, compassion and trustworthiness are all poetically illuminated for us in the Psalms. Every word penned emits the aroma of humble worship and reverential fear.

In the Psalms, we have been bequeathed a treasury of the most profound interactions between pious men and a loving, caring God. This 12-week study of the choicest Psalms takes you right into those intimate exchanges and evokes a determined desire to find His Presence for yourself.